CO-

POWERFUL PARTNERSHIPS
IN MARRIAGE

DR. DAN & LINDA WILSON
FOREWORD BY PATRICIA KING

Featuring: *Che & Sue Ahn, Joshua & Janet Mills,
Bart & Kim Hadaway, Dr. Paul & Teri Looney,
Steve and Marci Fish, Robert & Katie Souza*

ISBN: 978-1-936101-69-6

Published by XP Publishing, P. O. Box 1017 Maricopa, Arizona, 85139
www.XPPublishing.com
Printed in the United States of America. All rights reserved.

ENDORSEMENTS

I have longed for someone to write a book that teaches husbands and wives how they can live together as TWO powerful people. I was stunned by the practical application of how CO-reigning partners can empower each other to fulfill their own God-given destinies. As I read the Wilson's book, I had a crazy experience: the words of the manuscript emerged from the pages of this book and began to paint a beautiful portrait of intoxicated lovers wildly and passionately living together in celestial harmony. I had this sudden revelation that my own great 36-year marriage could take on a new heavenly dimension.

I began to understand that **CO- Powerful Partnerships in Marriage** is not just another book about marriage. It's a tour guide into a spiritual three-cord union that can open up a supernatural vortex over our holy relationships. This book could be a catalyst to relational transition that could launch our marriages into the great adventure in God. I highly recommend this book to every married couple and all those who are aspiring to be wed.

KRIS VALLOTTON

Co-Founder of Bethel School of Supernatural Ministry
Author of seven books including, **The Supernatural Ways of Royalty**
Senior Associate Leader of Bethel Church, Redding, California

In this book, you can see very clearly how God called for the two to walk together and become one. As a woman, I really appreciate Dan and Linda's heart as they are one in heart and spirit. I love that they exemplify what it is to be husband and wife but also **CO**-laborers. In this book you will have the veil removed from your way of thinking. It simply breaks down the Scriptures and really brings back to the body of Christ what it is to love and honor, which most of us have said in our marriage vows. I see it as the law of honor: what you don't give you will never have. A must read for those getting married. It will help jump-start and by-pass years of trying to figure one another out.

ANGELA T. GREENIG

President of Angela Greenig Ministries
Evangelist/Author

"**CO-**" is an interesting prefix. It is very simple and yet so complex. The word means together. COmmunicate. It takes at least two to COmmunicate. COdependency takes two again, people that depend on each other for their own needs to be met. COoperate takes two working together to make it happen. This book has many well known people working together to make this happen. It is based on true life stories of COuples—there is the **CO-** again—that have learned through experience how to work together for the same goal. This book will help you walk out your life with the COmpanion that God has sent you in a more fulfilling way. I would encourage you to read this book time and time again.

JOAN HUNTER

President Joan Hunter Ministries and Hunter Ministries
Evangelist/Author

God speaks out in every generation, mainly using men and women. Dr. Dan and Linda have a fresh anointing for bringing out a message for marriages in this generation.

I truly love and second the timeless, great insight shared in this new book, **CO- *Powerful Partnerships in Marriage***. It is a "must read."

JOHN RICHARD MUBIRU
Amen and Amen
Community Care Evangelistic Mission
Uganda

I had the joy and honor of being married to Michal Ann Goll for over 32 years before she graduated to her heavenly reward in the fall of 2008. We lived the message in this book. We helped to pioneer the message in this book. We were more than a married couple who had the joy of parenting four great kids together. We were each other's best coaches, cheerleaders and partners in ministry, taking the Good News around the world. Now it is other people's turn to pick up that baton and run their leg of the race. That is what the Wilsons are doing and that is what this book is all about. You will be inspired as a couple to be all that you can be in Christ Jesus and together release the sweet smelling fragrance of Christ wherever you go! It is an honor to commend to you **CO- *Powerful Partnerships In Marriage***.

JAMES W. GOLL
Encounters Network • Prayer Storm • Compassion Acts
National Best Selling Author

ACKNOWLEDGEMENTS

— **Jesus** — You are the ultimate example of submission. We honor You as King of kings and Lord of lords.

— **Our Six CO- Author Couples** — Thank you for being vulnerable and real. You are beautiful jewels shining brightly for the glory of our God! We love and respect each of you.

— **Ed Huston, PhD** — Your expertise in animal husbandry and biblical history certainly enhanced our story. We respect and honor you as a man of God and a leader at the city gates of San Angelo.

— **Carol Martinez** — We think you are an amazing woman of God! It is a wonderful gift to have you as both our publisher and as our friend. We love you!

— **Ryan Adair** — Thank you so much for once again blessing us with your editing skill. We appreciate your integrity with Scripture and your willingness to teach us as you work.

— **Michelle Burkett** — The peace and grace you carry has surrounded us as you have polished and copy edited this manuscript. Thanks for being our friend!

— **Jake Rossilli** — Thank you for your cover design. You are made in our Father's image, exhibiting kindness and creativity. We think you and Katie rock!

DEDICATION

Jason & Natalie,

    Marko & Megan...

        We see you living the life of **CO-**.

            We love you massively!

CONTENTS

PART ONE: Past Powerful Partnerships

PART TWO: Present Powerful Partnerships

FOREWORD

By Patricia King

ONE OF THE MOST vivid examples in Scripture of co-laboring for the glory of God is discovered in the story of Deborah (Judges 4). In this chapter we find the sons of Israel very distraught and severely oppressed. It was at this time in history that the Lord raised up Deborah both as a prophet and a judge. In those days, the people of God were not ruled by a king, they were governed by the word of the Lord through the prophets, while the law was enforced by the judges. Deborah held both of these important positions. The prophets and judges were not self-appointed, rather they were divinely appointed by God Himself.

Deborah was not the only strategically appointed individual in her day. Her husband's name was Lapidoth, which means "a burning torch." Deborah could not have done what she did without her Lapidoth (burning torch) supporting her. His position and function was as vital—and equally important—as Deborah's. Together, Deborah and Lapidoth fulfilled destiny. That is why Lapidoth's name was mentioned in the Scripture. You never hear his name again but he had an important role — significant enough to be mentioned. Deborah and Lapidoth were a team. Deborah and Lapidoth were **CO-**.

Of course, Deborah and Lapidoth did not walk or labor alone in their day. Barak was also divinely appointed to a strategic role. He was a powerful military officer who was trusted with thousands of troops. He was the head of the military but Barak so respected Deborah's role as the prophetess that he refused to go out to battle without her. He was insistent that the Word of God was carried into the battle (in those days, only the prophet could hear the Word of God for the nations).

And of course there was Jael. The battle could not have been completed without precious, faithful, Jael. The victory and the glory were secured by everyone CO-laboring, CO-honoring and CO-depending on each other. The victory and the glory were secured because there was mutual respect and trust as they made way for each other to function in their God-given gifts. They CO-labored and they CO-shared the victory.

In Christ, there is no male or female. There is neither Jew nor Gentile; bond or free. All are one in Christ. In Christ we identify gifts, callings and assignments in each other. The mystery of Christ in us the hope of glory is the essence of **CO-**. This insightful glimpse into the mystery of Christ in each other is especially vital within a marriage relationship.

Dr. Dan and Linda Wilson have discovered that secret and enjoy an impressive marriage relationship together in the Lord. They CO-seek Him; they CO-labor with Him and for Him; and they CO-love Him. I adore the wonderful example and model they set for all of us. They honor, love and respect each other as they walk together even though they are unique individuals, each beautifully designed to glorify the Lord. They are unique, yet they are **CO-**. Not only do they **CO-** with each other, but they also walk in **CO-** with others in the Body of Christ.

Their primary passion is to see couples CO-love, CO-honor, CO-labor and CO-enjoy the fullness of all Christ has called them to be and do. This passion pours out to those they come in contact with. I believe their book **CO- *Powerful Partnerships in Marriage***, with the variety of authors who have contributed to the content, will release vision, hope, encouragement and impartation to the reader. Not only will the reader see ways to walk in **CO-** in a marriage relationship, but also with others in the Body for strategic assignments.

May you be extremely blessed in both your marriage and God-given callings as you **CO-**!

INTRODUCTION

By Dr. Dan & Linda Wilson

THE CAR DOOR OPENED ABRUPTLY as our vehicle pulled up to a large metal gate. As instructed, we[1] moved quickly into the complex of buildings that a popular nightclub had abandoned only a decade ago. Western tourists were common in this sprawling Asian metropolis, but were rarely seen in this dilapidated part of town. It was important for us to avoid unnecessary attention.

We heard the delightful sound of praise songs being sung in another language as we walked across the courtyard. Our ears heard the music as we entered the classroom, but in our spirits we perceived pure and undefiled worship—worship that was pleasing to God. Our hearts were filled with excitement and joy as we joined with these thirty young men and women who had come to the ministry school in passionate pursuit of the Spirit of God and His truth.

---

[1] Since this book is written by both of us, Dr. Dan and Linda Wilson, we will be using "we" and "our" to refer to both of us throughout the entirety of the book, instead of the usual "I" and "my."

Attending the pastor training school was an act of faith on each of their parts. In spite of media reports suggesting increasing religious freedom in this communist country, the reality we discovered was that Christian evangelism remained highly illegal.[2] Serious persecution still threatened those who proclaimed Jesus Christ as Lord. The students came without the right to be there, risking arrest and imprisonment for the privilege of studying the Bible. Although so poor they had no funds to buy food for the coming day, they remained confident of having everything they needed for life and godliness.

Our mission that day was to share God's gloriously good plan for marital union that we refer to as "supernatural marriage." These future pastors and leaders of Asia received our message with joy and enthusiasm. None of them believed they had grown up in a family where their father and mother had truly loved each other. Only one of them had ever known of such a marriage among all their acquaintances. Still they knew it was God's intention that marriage would be filled with love, joy and oneness far exceeding what they had observed in society.

As we continued talking about marriage, God revealed to all of us that in His supernatural realm we are no longer restricted by the experiences of those who have gone before us. With access to God's miraculous transformation in our hearts, we can be released to fully enter the glorious plan to which we have been called.

---

[2] Real religious persecution still persists in much of Asia. It is not just a thing of the distant past—but a very present danger for anyone who names the name of Christ. Even though much of the media tries to portray that these countries allow religious freedom, the governments still attempt to tightly control Christian expression and activities. Serious consequences remain for anyone who pursues Christ in a non-government approved church.

Then came *the* question—the same one we have heard throughout the world as we share about God's plan for marriage. After visiting thirty-five countries on six different continents, it has become clear that Satan's attack on marriage leads to similar questions and problems in every culture. A young, single woman asked, "What about 'submission' in marriage?" The expression on her face revealed the confusion, frustration and angst from which the inquiry came. She had heard her father quote Ephesians 5:22 to her mother in an authoritative and controlling voice far too often: "*Wives, submit to your husbands as to the Lord.*" During her twenty years of life, she had seen this verse used by men to dominate and manipulate the women they had married. She could not relate to the wisdom and beauty of this portion of Scripture when she only understood it as a harsh tool used for the restraint of wives.

God's Word is Always Good

As Bill Johnson was speaking some time ago, he turned to a Scripture in his Bible and found it was far different from the one he intended to read. Slightly embarrassed but undeterred, he went on to read the unexpected passage. He then said, "That is not at all the verse I planned to use, but it is really quite good! In fact, everything in the Bible is good... even the Table of Contents!"

The truth is that Ephesians 5:22 is completely good. Unfortunately, it is often used as an excuse by domineering and manipulative men trying to abusively suppress their wives into obedience. The fact that it has been misunderstood and misapplied by many through the years does not take away from its intrinsic beauty, validity and potential value for us all. This verse Satan has intended to misuse for harm, God will correctly and triumphantly use for the glorious good of His people.

The kind of submission God desires to be demonstrated in our lives is a voluntary act, an honest expression of honor and respect. It enhances the realization of self-worth for both giver and receiver. Godly submission is *not* equal to capitulation and is free of manipulation. When we submit one to another, it must be consistent with the defining words of Colossians 3:18, *"as is fitting in the Lord."* It is a gift of honor that cannot be forced or required—a true act of *agape*[3] love.

In the following chapters of **CO- Powerful Partnerships in Marriage**, we will present a balanced and encouraging view of how spouses, who are co-heirs with Christ, can learn the true meaning of submission in their relationships with each other and God. Along with a theological examination of prominent married couples in the Bible, we will also have a little fun and take some liberty to present fictional representations of these powerful couples. We will use both of these methods to destroy the confusion and reveal the divine wisdom of this well-known passage from Ephesians.

---

[3] Dan helps define agape in *Supernatural Marriage: The Joy of Spirit-Led Intimacy*, where he writes: "The New Testament writers use the Greek word 'agape' to help explain the perfect love of God intended to flow through each person involved in marriage... In fact, by inspiring this glorious chapter defining agape love (referring to 1 Corinthians 13), God perfectly describes Himself. Agape love is the essence of who God is. It is the solid rock upon which holy matrimony is built.

"*Agape* is selfless and giving. Its motives are completely pure. *Agape* looks to the needs and desires of others in relationship with us and it demonstrates patience and kindness while wrapping its possessor in a cloak of humility. One who is filled with *agape* forgives easily, enabling the release of injuries from the past with a fully open hand. A spouse filled with the *agape* of God maintains hope even in situations where logic would dictate despair, knowing we will not be disappointed by hope..." (163).

In the second part of the book, six couples actively involved in Kingdom-ministry will share their personal testimonies of how God has taught them memorable lessons as to the value and significance of submission within marriage. We are confident that by the time you have finished reading **CO-**, Ephesians 5:22 will no longer be a source of confusion or frustration in your life. Instead, you will joyfully agree with Bill Johnson that God, and *every* part of God's Word, is good *all* the time.

Dan & Linda

Part One

Past Powerful Partnerships

Chapter 1

Deborah:
A Leader with
Strength & Peace

By Dr. Dan & Linda Wilson

*Deborah, a prophetess, the wife of Lappidoth, was lead-
ing Israel at that time. She held court under the Palm of
Deborah between Ramah and Bethel in the hill country
of Ephraim, and the Israelites came to her to have their
disputes decided. She sent for Barak son of Abinoam
from Kedesh in Naphtali and said to him, "The LORD,
the God of Israel, commands you: 'Go, take with you
ten thousand men of Naphtali and Zebulun and lead the
way to Mount Tabor. I will lure Sisera, the commander
of Jabin's army, with his chariots and his troops to the
Kishon River and give him into your hands …'"*

*When they told Sisera that Barak son of Abinoam
had gone up to Mount Tabor, Sisera gathered together*

his nine hundred iron chariots and all the men with him,
from Harosheth Haggoyim to the Kishon River.

Then Deborah said to Barak, "Go! This is the day
the LORD has given Sisera into your hands. Has not the
LORD gone ahead of you?" So Barak went down Mount
Tabor, followed by ten thousand men. At Barak's ad-
vance, the LORD routed Sisera and all his chariots and
army by the sword, and Sisera abandoned his chariot and
fled on foot ...

On that day God subdued Jabin, the Canaanite
king, before the Israelites. And the hand of the Israelites
grew stronger and stronger against Jabin, the Canaanite
king, until they destroyed him.

— Judges 4:4-7; 12-15; 23-24 —

Deborah's God-Given Wisdom

SHE WALKED WITH CONFIDENCE AND grace through the crowd of several hundred who gathered weekly around a distinctive, mature palm tree named in her honor. Palm trees were prized throughout Israel for their beauty, the delicious dates they produced and their ability to survive harsh conditions. Judging the people beneath its branches signified that Deborah was indeed the political and judicial "head" of Israel.[4] There was no doubt this powerful woman was both the leader and hero of her nation.

Through the heat of the day, Deborah would sit in the cool shade of the palm that bore her name. The first defendant to be brought before her that day was Gaddi. Assisted by his two sons, he raised sheep for a living in the nearby hill country of Ramah, just north of Jerusalem. Though this thirty-four-year-old father

---

[4] See Isaiah 9:14 & 19:15

had taken a bath before going to stand in front of the judge of Israel, he still smelled strongly of the animals he tended. The odor was common among the people, not offensive to either those officiating or to anyone else in the observing crowd. He came to defend himself against an accusation, a problem no one in his district had been able to solve. The crowd buzzed with excitement as they whispered details of the dilemma, waiting with anticipation to find out how the wisdom of God in Deborah would once again resolve a situation that seemed to have no good solution.

A few feet away stood the accuser, a middle-aged man with a full, black beard. He angrily glared at Gaddi while pointing a trembling finger in his face. With fire in his eyes, Reu shouted, "This is the man who stole my sheep! For generations his family's animals have all had white heads. Everyone knows that my sheep are famous for having black heads and very fat tails—extra fat for surviving the harshest of times. Terah and Abram brought them here long ago when they left Ur of the Chaldeans. Now my unfaithful neighbor has six sheep with heads that are clearly black. And none of his other sheep have fat tails! It is obvious that he stole them from my herd!"

Gaddi, with his head bowed in humility and shame, used few words in his defense. In an emotional voice he responded, "The sheep my family raises are the best in Ramah—straight legs, thick muscles and long, fine wool. But the six new animals are the finest I have ever seen. They are bigger and healthier than any sheep in Israel. And they have fat tails to boot! I have no idea how my ewes produced them. Yet I swear to all of you standing here today, not one of them is stolen!"

Asking for silence in the assembly, Deborah brought the two men before her and intently looked into their eyes for over a minute. She could sense an element of pride in the accuser and recognized the essence of honesty shown by humility in the accused. The leader of Israel closed her eyes for a few seconds, gathering her thoughts. Breaking the silence, she gave her decision in the matter with strength and authority.

Speaking as an oracle of the Lord, this wise judge proclaimed, "God has given clear resolution to this dilemma. Neither plaintiff nor defendant has brought deception to my court this day." Then she explained how a black-headed ram from the flocks of Reu had briefly escaped and bred with ewes in Gaddi's flock. The lambs produced were truly amazing, with the best attributes of both types of sheep evident in each animal. The new breed of sheep that resulted was the best that had ever been seen in Ephraim, a magnificent gift arranged by the astounding God of Israel.

Deborah went on to instruct that Gaddi and Reu were to share rams each spring and interbreed their flocks for a period of seven years. The new and better breed of sheep produced would be distributed to every tribe in Israel, blessing the entire nation with greater prosperity for generations to come. It was a brilliant solution to a problem that had upset the families of both men for nearly a year. Both parties left the assembly in peace, amazed at the wisdom of their judge's decision. God had again shown grace and kindness through Deborah to all of His beloved people.

Wife, Mother & Woman of Prominence

Deborah carried within her astonishing gifts from God—most likely receiving her gifting as prophetess and judge directly from the "*Spirit of the Lord.*" The book of Judges clearly states this to be the case for Othniel[5] before her, as well as Gideon,[6]

---

[5] Judges 3:10
[6] Judges 6:34

Jephthah[7] and Samson[8] after her. Not only did the Holy Spirit enable Deborah to extend peace to individuals and groups coming to her as she sat under the Palm of Deborah, but she literally imparted supernatural peace to an entire nation. There was something about this peace that was beyond human understanding, clearly originating within the supernatural realm of God.

Deborah literally imparted supernatural peace to an entire nation.

Deborah lived a life worthy of the respect she gracefully carried. Men and women would come from all over Israel, walking many days in pursuit of an opportunity to share their struggles with her and receive the wisdom they needed in dealing with the frustrations of daily life. She carried weighty authority from God that impacted every person she encountered. Her life was a blessing to the nation she led.

She is the only individual leader of Israel described in the Bible who is not male. It was very rare for women to rise to great prominence in her day. It is still unusual thirty-two hundred years later in our own time. There was no record of royalty in her lineage. She did not reach her position through a coup, an assassination, or by carefully obtaining political advantage over those who opposed her. What enabled her, even as a woman, to ascend to the highest position in Israel? What lessons would God wish to teach us through her unique and distinctly successful life?

Even though Deborah was a prophetess, a judge and the leader of a nation—decisive and correct in her proclamations,

[7] Judges 11:29
[8] Judges 13:25

victorious in battle—she was also a mother[9] and is described as *"the wife of Lappidoth."*[10] There is no criticism against Deborah written in Scripture, yet her position of authority and acts of leadership seem very different than the misguided interpretation of Ephesians 5:22: "Wives, submit to your husbands as to the Lord." This Scripture is primarily referenced by those who strive to prevent women from assuming positions of influence within the Kingdom of God. Yet, there is no contradiction between the Old and New Testaments regarding the issue of submission within marriage. We believe Deborah and her husband were mutually submissive to one another while she carried the power and authority to lead a nation.

The God who brought Deborah to such a prominent position among His chosen people is the same triune God who long before described Himself as "I AM" in the burning bush to Moses,[11] later showing Himself to the world through the incarnation as Jesus,[12] and now empowers His children through the promised Holy Spirit.[13] Clearly, the truths of God do not change with the seasons or the years. We are reminded that Jesus, who is the visible demonstration of God's essence, remains *"the same yesterday and today and forever."*[14] Deborah beautifully demonstrated God's perfect plan for women of faith throughout the ages. What was best in the eyes of God for Deborah thirty-two centuries ago is no different than what is best for the woman of today.

---

[9] See Judges 5:7
[10] Judges 4:4
[11] See Exodus 3:14
[12] See John 1:14
[13] See Acts 2:33 & Ephesians 1:13
[14] Hebrews 13:8

Deborah - Authority with Peace

The authority Deborah comfortably carried is seen as she spoke a prophetic command to Barak. She declared, *"The LORD, the God of Israel, commands you: 'Go, take with you ten thousand men of Naphtali and Zebulun and lead the way to Mount Tabor. I will lure Sisera, the commander of Jabin's army, with his chariots and his troops to the Kishon River and give him into your hands.'"*[15] Barak, later to be recognized in the book of Hebrews as a man of great faith,[16] received the word of the Lord and immediately acted upon it. The result of Barak's obedience was that the Holy Spirit led Sisera and his army into a trap in the valley below Mount Tabor. The ensuing defeat was a crushing blow to the military forces under Jabin, ultimately leading to a complete destruction of his kingdom.

Following this immense victory came forty years of peace. A single battle is not sufficient to maintain peace within a nation for this length of time. Deborah was much more than an army commander. She carried the supernatural essence of peace within her spirit and soul. It was a spiritual gift freely given by God and graciously received by her. During her years of leading Israel, this peace manifested within Deborah's people because she extended it to them in much the same way as God extended it to her.

Peace is a covenant sign of a supernatural marriage.

We believe Deborah, as a married woman, would not have experienced peace in its fullness, or shared it with her nation in

---

[15] Judges 4:6
[16] See Hebrews 11:32

the way that she did, if it had not been characteristic of her marriage with Lappidoth. Peace is a covenant sign of a supernatural marriage.[17] The fact that peace persisted is evidence that her marriage relationship was also filled with the lasting peace that can only come from God. She could not have brought true peace to Israel if there had been strife and rebellion within her home.

Samson - Strength Without Peace

Like Deborah, Samson was a powerful judge over Israel.[18] But Samson did not honor God with a healthy marriage relationship. Although given authority, power and responsibility similar to that conferred upon Deborah, Samson did not possess true peace and therefore could not bring a covering of peace to the nation of Israel. He carried rebellion within his heart and shared it with others wherever he went, leading to a life filled with strife, betrayal and tragedy.[19] His sinful relationship with Delilah is one of several examples of imprudence, eventually leading to catastrophic consequences in his life.

In spite of his recurrent rebellion, Samson was enabled by God to be the centerpiece of a huge victory for Israel against the Philistines in Gaza. We believe his heart's desire was to honor the Lord, but his road to triumph was paved with capture, torture, blindness, enslavement and eventual death. Samson rebelled against God's plan for marriage and bequeathed strife to his people. But Deborah honored God through her marriage, and the inheritance of her people was forty years of blissful peace.

---

[17] See Dan Wilson, *Supernatural Marriage: The Joy of Spirit-Led Intimacy*, (XP Publishing, 2010), 169-170.

[18] You can read the account of Samson in Judges 13:1–16:31.

[19] This can be seen in Samson revealing the secret of his strength to Delilah (Judges 16:6-22), marrying a woman in rebellion against his parents' wishes (Judges 14:1-7), spending the night with a prostitute (Judges 16:1-2), breaking the Nazarite vow by getting honey out of dead animal carcass (Judges 14:8-9), and culminating in his death (Judges 16:23-31).

Some would say that Lappidoth must have been a weak man for his wife to have shown such strength as a leader of Israel. We are confident the opposite is true. The most reliable way for a wife to become strong is for her husband to consistently encourage her to put her God-given authority into action. Only a man who is strong himself can successfully play this enabling role. A weak husband will drain his wife's strength because of his own fear and insecurity. A husband who has been made strong by the Lord will prophetically see his wife's Kingdom-destiny, joyfully help her enter into it and fully release her to do exactly that for which she was created. Deborah's husband Lappidoth was this kind of man.

A Lesson from Drafting

When flying in their familiar V pattern, geese will "draft" off of the adjacent bird slightly ahead in the formation. This instinctual habit makes the flying a little easier, improving each bird's chance of surviving the long migration. The lead goose has no partner to draft from and faces the wind alone. Even the strongest of geese cannot permanently hold this position. For the journey to be successful, another bird must take over the hardest flying for a time, allowing the previous leader to rest—only later to take the lead again.

This sharing of responsibility is characteristic of all good marriages. Deborah seemed to take the lead much more often than the typical wife. Undoubtedly, there were times Lappidoth was led by God to go in front and allow his wife to draft off of his strong flying while she rested. The division of responsibility required for a marriage relationship to be healthy is completely consistent with what we read in Ecclesiastes 4:9-10:

Two are better than one,
because they have a good return for their work:
If one falls down,
his friend can help him up.
But pity the man who falls
and has no one to help him up!

No marriage partner is so strong as to never need to be helped up by the other. Unquestionably, it is best when both husband and wife realize their own inner strength. It is vitally important that each partner be prepared to take the lead when the other enters a time of extreme need. For the marriage to be truly great, both partners must be strong.

What shifts a marriage from great to astounding, however, is the addition of the third strand described a couple of verses later: *"Though one may be overpowered, two can defend themselves. A cord of three strands is not quickly broken."*[20]

> The most reliable way for a wife to become strong is for her husband to consistently encourage her to put her God-given authority into action.

Spouses who host the presence and power of the Holy Spirit in the center of their relationship are shifted into a new level of marital pleasure, strength and effectiveness. This transfer into a higher degree of functioning is not accomplished by human strength or struggle. It occurs almost effortlessly through intimately relating with God, spirit to Spirit. Deborah and her husband enjoyed an early example of supernatural

---

[20] Ecclesiastes 4:12

marriage.[21] Led by a desire to submit to God, they also submitted to each other. Through supernatural submission, they lived victorious lives filled with peace, fully accomplishing the destiny for which they were created.

> For the marriage to be truly great, both partners must be strong.

Married women today have opportunities that mirror those of Deborah. All have been called and have access to power that releases victory over the enemies of God. His peace can be enjoyed for a lifetime. What you bring into your marriage is a manifestation of who you are on the inside. Who you are dramatically affects the relational tone of your life—experiences with your spouse, family and all others you encounter. Like Deborah, you function as a conduit, bringing either a culture of peace or strife into your family. What is carried within you will influence all those who know you, for evil or for good. Do not underestimate the significance of who you are and what you choose to carry. Always choose peace.

Societal Role Restrictions

Though much progress has been made in certain cultures, every nation on earth is still predominantly controlled by the men who live within it. Deborah lived in a male-dominated society, but was chosen by God to show all future generations the potential strength and effectiveness of a wife intimately connected with the King of Glory. It is our belief that one reason God allowed Deborah to function consistently and successfully

---

[21] See Dan Wilson, *Supernatural Marriage: The Joy of Spirit-Led Intimacy*, (XP Publishing, 2010), 22.

throughout her years as judge over Israel was that her marriage relationship brought honor to Him.

There may always be societal restrictions in the roles wives are encouraged and allowed to play. But the life of Deborah reminds us that our gracious Father is much more focused on releasing His children than holding them back. Regardless of gender, His intentions for us are far bigger than we realize. Male or female, slave or free,[22] God is ready to astound us all with the magnificence of His plans. As co-heirs with Christ, both wives and husbands walk together in power and supernatural confidence toward the destinies placed before them. Submitting to each other and to God, we can live lives filled with supernatural peace, blessing our marriage, family, culture and the world in which we live.

---

[22] See Galatians 3:28

Chapter 2

Proverbs 31: A Prophetic Model

By Dr. Dan & Linda Wilson

A wife of noble character who can find?
She is worth far more than rubies.
Her husband has full confidence in her
and lacks nothing of value.
She brings him good, not harm,
all the days of her life.
She selects wool and flax
and works with eager hands.
She is like the merchant ships,
bringing her food from afar.
She gets up while it is still dark;
she provides food for her family
and portions for her servant girls.
She considers a field and buys it;

out of her earnings she plants a vineyard.
She sets about her work vigorously;
her arms are strong for her tasks.
She sees that her trading is profitable,
and her lamp does not go out at night.
In her hand she holds the distaff
and grasps the spindle with her fingers.
She opens her arms to the poor
and extends her hands to the needy.
When it snows, she has no fear for her household;
for all of them are clothed in scarlet.
She makes coverings for her bed;
she is clothed in fine linen and purple.
Her husband is respected at the city gate,
where he takes his seat among the elders of the land.
She makes linen garments and sells them,
and supplies the merchants with sashes.
She is clothed with strength and dignity;
she can laugh at the days to come.
She speaks with wisdom,
and faithful instruction is on her tongue.
She watches over the affairs of her household
and does not eat the bread of idleness.
Her children arise and call her blessed;
her husband also, and he praises her:
"Many women do noble things,
but you surpass them all."
Charm is deceptive, and beauty is fleeting;
but a woman who fears the LORD *is to be praised.*
Give her the reward she has earned,
and let her works bring her praise at the city gate.

— Proverbs 31:10-31 —

A Tale of Love & Honor

I
T WAS A QUARTER OF SIX ON Thursday morning in the city of Shechem, Manasseh. Moshe was awakened abruptly by the crowing of his neighbor's newest and loudest rooster. He smiled when he saw that he was alone in the bed. Anna, his wife of twenty-four years, had gotten up earlier than usual to be sure the servant girls were preparing the special breakfast planned to begin this momentous day.

The couple had decided years ago that the large vineyard in the valley below their house could be a wonderful asset that would provide both work and income for their growing family. The two older boys were now married and starting to have children of their own. Their daughters were not yet betrothed, but the time for that would be coming soon enough. After years of saving and months of planning, this was the day for Moshe to have final discussions with the vineyard owner, come to an ultimate agreement and purchase the land. Full of excitement he jumped from the bed and rushed downstairs to greet his family.

Breakfast was magnificent that morning with freshly baked bread, sliced tomatoes, cucumbers, olives and salted fish. Anna treated Moshe like a king in a palace. He loved his wife deeply, often telling his friends that she was the finest and kindest woman he had ever met. These two often affirmed each other with words spoken from the heart, neither intended nor received as flattery. Anna and the girls laughed at Moshe across the breakfast table. They had never seen him this full of joy so early in the morning. Excitement swept through the entire home that day. The land they had worked for and prayed about for years would soon be theirs.

Suddenly, there was a loud knock at the door. Invited in, a messenger rushed to the table where Moshe's family was eating. Gasping for breath he shouted, "There is an extremely urgent situation that involves the life or death of a young man from Bethel! All the elders of Shechem are needed immediately! You must join them now at the city gate!" At first Moshe was frustrated, even aggravated at the unexpected call to service. It was the husband's job to oversee business transactions for the family. Completing the deal for the vineyard today was vitally important, but how could he not respond to a true emergency at the gates of his city? The people of Shechem trusted him and needed him at critical times such as this.

Nearly a minute of complete silence in the room was broken by Anna's bold and confident proclamation: "There is no option for you, my darling. You must go to the city gate. I will complete the deal and purchase the vineyard as we had planned. Tonight we will celebrate together." In mere moments, the expression on Moshe's face dramatically changed from consternation to one of serenity, revealing the surprising peace that had just entered his heart.

When Moshe saw the other elders at the gate, they surrounded an eighteen-year-old man named Simeon. His story was difficult to understand because he cried uncontrollably. The previous afternoon he had been helping a master mason build a tall wall for a wealthy family in Bethel. Without warning, a portion of the wall collapsed, falling on the man who had hired him for the day, immediately killing him. When the family of the dead mason heard what had happened, they accused Simeon of murder and threatened to stone him. Barely escaping, he had run through the night without stopping and just reached the city of refuge before he collapsed in complete exhaustion.

After interviewing Simeon and meeting together for two hours of discussion and prayer, the elders decided the man was guilty of manslaughter, not murder. He would be allowed to live out his days as a refugee in their city. It would not be safe for him to leave town until the death of the high priest, but no one could enter the city of refuge with the intent to harm him. A wise and merciful decision had been made that day by Moshe and the elders of Shechem. Simeon's life was spared.

Upon returning home late in the afternoon, Moshe found his family and servants in the midst of a joyful celebration. Anna had perfectly performed what was normally the task of a husband. The deal she made was even better than they had expected. Both land and vineyard could now be fully enjoyed by their family till the next Year of Jubilee, three decades away. Anna had submitted to her husband's need to faithfully do his duty as an elder of the city. Moshe submitted to his wife by allowing her to use her talents in an unusual way to purchase land that would bless their family for another generation. With love and respect they had truly honored each other that day. They went to bed that night full of joy and contentment. The peace of God covered them like a blanket as they drifted off to sleep.

Beautiful Dance of Submission

The woman described in Proverbs 31 had many qualities and characteristics that mirror the portrayal of Deborah in Judges 4 and 5. In this familiar chapter, Solomon,[23] a man possessing supernatural wisdom, paints a picture of the ideal Jewish wife. His depiction of her often surprises those who read it because she is capable of doing things far beyond the typical cultural expectations for wives. At first, this degree of authority and independence from a husband might seem to contradict Paul's command that wives "*submit*"[24] to their husbands. Nothing could be further from the truth. As we unpack hidden treasures from these verses,

---

[23] King Lemuel of Proverbs 31:1 is believed to be another name for King Solomon.

[24] Ephesians 5:22

the wisdom and appropriateness of a married woman living a life full of accomplishment will be seen. For a godly wife, this is her planned and even expected destiny.

> A woman ...
> will sometimes
> appear to be
> a Proverbs 31 wife
> on the outside,
> while her
> true inner-self
> is something
> altogether different.

We read that a noble wife finds, buys, develops and profits from agricultural land.[25] She works hard, sometimes long into the night—making her physically strong and bringing financial benefit to the family. Apparently she pursues these business ventures with significant independence from her husband, a reversal of the traditional roles in marriage.

On the other hand, in several unhealthy marriages we observed that a wife's new activity in business was actually a warning sign of marital strife. A woman with an independent and rebellious spirit will sometimes appear to be a Proverbs 31 wife on the outside, while her true inner-self is something altogether different. Her husband is forced to passively watch as she controls more and more areas within the marriage that he knows should be in his realm of authority. This control by coercion can be demeaning and discouraging, leading to the husband feeling a deep sense of personal impotence.

It is traditional for husbands to have major input into large financial decisions that affect the entire family. Both men and women can have a strong business sense, but a wife who refuses to submit to her husband's desire to be directly involved in this area of finance may weaken his feelings of self-worth and damage the

---

[25] See Proverbs 31:16

strength of their emotional bond. In a similar vein, the husband who insists on always following the gender-specific traditions of society, simply because they are the norm, could be disobeying God and preventing his wife from reaching her full potential as a godly woman.

There are times a husband must be willing to give up his personal desires in order to accomplish what is best for all involved. A man of God will submit to the leading of the Holy Spirit and to his wife by allowing her to use her divinely acquired talents in ways that would most bless the family. Husband and wife are both called by God to do their jobs with commitment and excellence, even when what they have been called to does not match the expectation of others. Both spouses must be willing to submit to the wise and ultimately perfect plan of God if it is to be fully accomplished in their lives.

> A man of God will submit to the leading of the Holy Spirit and to his wife by allowing her to use her divinely aquired talents in ways that would most bless the family.

In Proverbs 31, the husband was called by God to take his seat among the elders at the city gate. He served the city in this position of honor and authority by helping make major decisions regarding its management, defense and plans for how future needs could be met. At the gate of a city of refuge he would be part of deciding whether a person from out of town who took another's life was guilty of murder or manslaughter. His decision literally meant life or death to the one asking to enter the city of refuge.[26]

---

[26] See Joshua 20:1-4

The number and weight of such decisions resulted in great respect among the people for this godly man. He was a trusted leader of his land, but this honorable job required much of his time. His Proverbs 31 wife submitted to his need to fulfill this God-given task by taking care of many of his normal duties as a husband. He also submitted to his wife by releasing her to use the gifts God had provided her with to do a wonderful job of accomplishing what he could not. Both spouses were fully submitting to God and to each other—a beautiful dance choreographed by the One who made them one.

Assigning Work Roles

In healthy marriages, husband and wife frequently discuss the needs of the family. They honestly look at their individual, God-given talents and ask for supernatural wisdom to know how best to use them to complete the tasks at hand. The opinions of others outside their marriage should be heard and prayerfully considered, but do not need to be followed when differing from the opinion of the two who think as one in the Lord. It is generally true to say that if both partners are at peace with God and truly at peace with each other, their major life decisions will be well made.

Always do what is best, not what is easiest.

For a marriage to be successful, it must be built upon mutual honor and submission. Regarding the process of assigning work roles within a marriage, the following points are recommended:

- Pray together and discuss each partner's giftings, interests, goals and expectations for a healthy marriage.

- Ask for the Spirit of Wisdom[27] as you initially assign spe-

---

[27] See Isaiah 11:2

cific, independent and shared roles.

- Continue being honest with each other as to whether or not you think the plan is working.

- Feel free to make suggestions of how roles might change for the better.

- Do not allow selfishness to prevent change.

- Always do what is best, not what is easiest.

- Never fear change.

- Encourage your mate to pursue their life-dreams whenever possible.

- Embrace abundant life now. Do not delay needed changes too far into the future.

- Verbally express *full confidence*[28] to your partner. Do not second-guess a decision made by your spouse when functioning in their assigned role. Suggest ways of improvement, but never criticize.

The husband of a Proverbs 31 wife has *"full confidence in her"*[29] and *"praises her."*[30] Spoken words of confidence and praise are greatly encouraging to both men and women. Words are powerful in their ability to either build up or break down a marriage partner. As Jesus said in the Sermon on the Mount: *"Don't pick on people, jump on their failures, criticize their faults—unless, of course, you want the same treatment. That critical spirit has a way of boomeranging."*[31] Fortunately, words of confidence and praise also have a way of coming back to the one who speaks them. What a blessing it is when they are returned!

---

[28] Proverbs 31:11
[29] *ibid*
[30] Proverbs 31:28
[31] Matthew 7:1 (The Message)

A Proverbs 31 Wife of Today

The wife described in Proverbs 31 surprises us! She lives above our expectations in every area of life while her family remains in perfect balance. Was this possible in 1200 BC? Is it even achievable for the woman, wife and mother of today? If so, then how can this be done?

For the past nineteen years, we have known a woman who, as a wife and mother, is well described by the words we read in this well-known Proverb. Rachel Beaver loves the church of which she is a charter member, but her vision and energies extend far beyond the church walls. As co-founder of House of Faith Ministries[32] in San Angelo, Texas, she helps lead an organization that utilizes volunteers from forty-two local churches who bring Back Yard Bible Clubs to thirteen hundred children every week. Rachel is loved by Christians throughout the region and honored by secular organizations for helping reduce crime in every part of the community.

> ...Mutual submission cannot occur in the natural realm of man ... it can only occur in the supernatural realm of God.

This woman of God loves to be home but is rarely there. In spite of the time demands coming from both business and ministry commitments, Rachel focuses on being intimate and sweet in her family relationships. They all know she will be there at the times when they need her most. The children honored Rachel when they were young; and as adults, they still honor her today. Working alongside Rachel in life and ministry is her husband,

---

[32] www.HOFministries.org

Bob, the pastor of their church and an elder to the city. His calling is very different from hers, yet their lives flow together with mutual honor and co-submission, in much the same way as the couple described in Proverbs 31. They work hard, play hard and are praised by all who know them. Bob and Rachel are lifetime lovers and the very best of friends.

With little effort we could tell you the stories of a dozen such wives and husbands we personally know. They exemplify the same quality of character and solid commitment that God desires to see in us all. The Bride of Christ will be resplendent in her beauty when she is full of wives and husbands such as these.

The Key to Effectiveness

The key to accomplishing all God has for us is found in Proverbs 31:30, where we learn that she is *"a woman who fears the* LORD*."* For both husband and wife, this is the essential first step toward accomplishing what needs to be done. When we fear the Lord, we quickly learn the value of submission to His will. Submitting to God, we obey His command to *"submit to one another out of reverence for Christ."*[33] Husband and wife are co-heirs with Christ. Their mutual submission cannot occur in the natural realm of man. It is a miraculous, Spirit-led event that can only occur in the supernatural realm of God.

When we submit to the desires of God and the needs of our partner in marriage, His Spirit enters and remains at the center of the union. Husband and wife are thus enabled to accomplish things in their life together that far exceed human capacity. The astonishingly effectual lives of the man and woman described in Proverbs 31 is a prophetic model that shows us the true potential

---

[33] Ephesians 5:21

of supernatural marriage. But the fulfillment of this seemingly impossible marital destiny only becomes possible when husband and wife submit daily to both God and one another. The supernatural wind of the Spirit will blow them exactly where they are intended to go.

Chapter 3

Priscilla & Aquila:
Supernatural Oneness

By Dr. Dan & Linda Wilson

After this, Paul left Athens and went to Corinth. There he met a Jew named Aquila, a native of Pontus, who had recently come from Italy with his wife Priscilla, because Claudius had ordered all Jews to leave Rome ...

Paul stayed on in Corinth for some time. Then he left the brothers and sisters and sailed for Syria, accompanied by Priscilla and Aquila. Before he sailed, he had his hair cut off at Cenchreae because of a vow he had taken. They arrived at Ephesus, where Paul left Priscilla and Aquila. He himself went into the synagogue and reasoned with the Jews ...

Meanwhile a Jew named Apollos, a native of Alexandria, came to Ephesus. He was a learned man, with a thorough knowledge of the Scriptures. He had been instructed in the way of the Lord, and he spoke with great *fervor and taught about Jesus accurately, though he knew only the baptism of John. He began to speak boldly in the synagogue. When Priscilla and Aquila heard him, they invited him to their home and explained to him the way of God more adequately.*

— Acts 18:1-2; 18-19; 24-26 —

The churches in the province of Asia send you greetings. Aquila and Priscilla greet you warmly in the Lord, and so does the church that meets at their house.

— 1 Corinthians 16:19-20 —

Greet Priscilla and Aquila, my fellow workers in Christ Jesus. They risked their lives for me. Not only I but all the churches of the Gentiles are grateful to them. Greet also the church that meets at their house.

— Romans 16:3-5a —

Greet Priscilla and Aquila and the household of Onesiphorus.

— 2 Timothy 4:19 —

An Ephesian's Letter to Paul

AQUILA, MINISTER OF THE GOSPEL with the church at Ephesus — To Paul, an apostle of Christ Jesus by the will of God: Grace, mercy and unending peace be yours from the Father, Son and Holy Spirit.

Two months have now passed since you left Ephesus to visit the churches of Jerusalem and Antioch. Priscilla and I miss you greatly, but know you must go where the Spirit leads. You, brother Paul, are very dear to our hearts.

We were talking just yesterday of that difficult time, forty-nine years after the death of our Savior, when Claudius ordered all Jews to immediately leave Rome.[34] Though the intentions of his edict were cruel, God blessed us through it by guiding us eastward to Corinth where we met you. We invited you to live with us above the shop in our home, thinking you could help us make tents. All along you knew the real reason we were brought together was that you would make us disciples of Jesus Christ. What a wondrous and joyful occasion it was that night you led us to Jesus! Our lives were forever changed.

Another special memory was the night when the synagogue leader, Crispus, and his entire family became believers in the Lord Jesus.[35] Priscilla and I looked at each other in amazement as we witnessed these prominent people receiving salvation just as we had a few weeks before. Truly, our God is no respecter of persons. He desires to reveal Himself to all who seek Him.

After the conversion of Crispus, many of the Jews became believers in Jesus. Do you remember the night we were baptizing and the line kept growing longer and longer? It reminded Priscilla of God multiplying the loaves and fishes by the Sea of Galilee. We finally went home well after midnight, joyfully exhausted and completely astounded. Only our living God can do such things!

Following this glorious event, persecution against the three of us increased from the non-believing Jews. It encouraged us all when Jesus spoke to you in that vision saying, *"Do not be afraid; keep on speaking, do not be silent. For I am with you, and no one is going to attack and harm you, because I have many people in this city."*[36] We accepted what you saw and trusted God would protect us all from harm.

[34] See Acts 18:1-4
[35] See Acts 18:8
[36] Acts 18:9-10

Soon after the vision, the Jews of Corinth brought you to court. Before you could even speak a word of defense, Gallio released you and drove them off. The crowd was so angry they attacked Sosthenes, their own leader, instead of you.[37] I'll have to admit that it was hard not to laugh when they turned on him.

Priscilla and I can sense in the Spirit that there is more persecution coming to you, brother Paul. But there is no reason to fear. God's plan is to bless you, not to harm you. He who began a good work in you will carry it on to completion.[38] My wife and I are confident that these words you have often spoken to others are true for yourself as well.

God truly blessed the time we worked together in Corinth. Not only did Jews come to know Jesus, but many followers of Aphrodite[39] also received the revelation of Jesus as the source of true love and fulfillment in life. It was such a blessing that Silas and Timothy were able to join us, bringing money to you that was donated by the churches in Macedonia. Their gift has made it possible for you to work full-time in ministry. It also did much to enable my wife and me to accept God's clear call to Ephesus. Church leadership in the region of Achaia has been left in trustworthy hands.

Do you remember the excitement we felt as the three of us first saw the amphitheater and fine library of Ephesus while slowly entering her shallow harbor? The moment we stepped off the boat, you began proclaiming, "Jesus is Lord of this city" with such enthusiasm and boldness that we were all taken aback. Together, we shared the revelation that it was not Artemis,[40] but Jesus that came from heaven to earth for the purpose of blessing all people.

---

[37] See Acts 18:12-17
[38] See Philippians 1:6
[39] In the first century, Corinth was a major center for the worship of Aphrodite, the Greek goddess of love and beauty.
[40] See Acts 19:35

After you sailed toward Jerusalem, an Alexandrian believer named Apollos arrived in Ephesus. His heart was pure and his doctrine accurate, but the message was incomplete because he had not yet experienced Spirit baptism.[41] Rather than correct Apollos in public, I invited him to visit with us in our home where we could explain the way of God more adequately.

At first, Apollos was surprised and a little hurt that he had misunderstood something so vitally important. Then, after listening to us talk for some time, Priscilla joined into our conversation. She spoke to Apollos with amazing wisdom and divine clarity. The gentleness God has placed in Priscilla was so valuable in the remainder of our time together. Her words were full of kindness and encouragement. The comments she made were key to Apollos' desiring and receiving the baptism of the Holy Spirit. You would have been so proud of her!

A few days after our evening together, Apollos crossed the Aegean Sea to minister in Corinth and the region of Achaia. We hear that he now teaches with greatly increased authority and power. The transformation of this godly man when he became more intimately connected with the Holy Spirit has truly been astonishing!

The believers here in Ephesus have a very good understanding of repentance and the water baptism John taught, but few are even aware that the Holy Spirit exists! When they hear about the Spirit, it is still difficult for them to receive this baptism because they cannot understand it with their minds. God's ways seem so illogical to those brought up in the teaching of the Athenian philosophers. I am hoping that during your next visit to Asia you might spend more time with us here. It would be wonderful if you could help the Ephesians get beyond the limitations of their

---

[41] See Acts 18:25

minds and learn the ways of the Spirit. Together, we could impart these wondrous gifts through the laying on of hands.

Before closing, I must tell you how thankful I am that you brought Priscilla and me with you to Ephesus. We felt so rejected during the persecution in Rome. There were moments we even thought God might have forgotten us. But in His perfect plan, He led us to Corinth where we would soon meet you and be led into relationship with our Lord Jesus! Great healing occurred during our time together, as well as important preparation for this next season of our lives.

Priscilla and I have found our marriage to be a powerful tool in ministry here in Ephesus. Our relationship is built around the unending love of God and empowered by the literal presence of His glory in us. The people here have never seen a marriage like ours, where two individuals have truly become one. To the Ephesians, our oneness is a miraculous sign and a wonder.

You, Paul, have helped Priscilla and me encounter God in ways that have changed how we think, live and love as we relate to those around us. Your teaching has even changed the way we relate to each other within our marriage. Many times you have reminded us that we are co-heirs with Christ and that we are called to submit to one another out of reverence for Him. We have remained unified in the Spirit through our marital bond of peace.

A wonderful legacy remains behind you in Asia as you celebrate Passover this spring in Jerusalem. We look forward with great anticipation to your planned return to visit the church in Ephesus. You are loved and appreciated by all who know and serve the Truth.

The church that meets in our home sends you their warmest greetings. Our love for you is rich and eternal because it comes from Christ Jesus our Lord. Amen.

The Two Become One Flesh

Priscilla and Aquila are mentioned seven times in four different New Testament books. Aquila is mentioned first only twice;[42] Priscilla is listed ahead of her husband five times and appears to be the better known of the two spouses. This is important because in the Bible the most prominent member of a ministry team is typically listed first. Using the duo of Paul and Barnabas as an example: Barnabas is listed first in Antioch[43] and Jerusalem,[44] where he was better established than Paul; while Paul's name is listed first when they were working together in a region of Asia, where he was the better known of the two.[45]

Although a woman, it is obvious that Priscilla had significant impact as a person and as a minister wherever this amazing couple lived. Both husband and wife were very influential in the development of the early church as they ministered together in the leading cities of Corinth, Ephesus and later, Rome.

The most remarkable thing about Priscilla and Aquila is that neither is ever mentioned alone in Scripture. It is as if those who knew them thought of them as a single entity and would always speak their names together in the same breath. In unity they served the King in His Kingdom, one in body, soul and spirit.[46] These partners were in submission to both God and each other. They had become true co-heirs in Christ. In every aspect of life and ministry their relationship satisfied the intended destiny of *"one flesh."*[47] Oneness was the key that allowed them to experience abundant life and an extremely productive ministry.

---

[42] This only occurs in Acts 18:2 & 1 Corinthians 16:19.

[43] See Acts 11:26

[44] See Acts 12:25

[45] See Acts 14:23

[46] Dan Wilson, *Supernatural Marriage: The Joy of Spirit-Led Intimacy*, (XP Publishing, 2010), 24.

[47] This phrase is recorded in Genesis 2:24.

Oneness was the key that allowed them to experience abundant life and an extremely productive ministry.

Paul, Apollos, Aquila and Priscilla had been co-laborers in establishing the church at Ephesus, which was healthy and strong. During his imprisonment in Rome, Paul wrote a letter to the Ephesians with great emphasis on the value of oneness.

I urge you to live a life worthy of the calling you have received. Be completely humble and gentle; be patient, bearing with one another in love. Make every effort to keep the unity of the Spirit through the bond of peace. There is one body and one Spirit, just as you were called to one hope when you were called; one Lord, one faith, one baptism; one God and Father of all, who is over all and through all and in all.

— Ephesians 4:1b-6 —

Paul's emphasis on unity and oneness came out of direct revelation from God. But it was also deeply rooted in the Old Testament Scriptures he knew so well. Oneness is a central, vital, eternal principle that is inherent to the character and divine plan of God. Moses declared this axiomatic truth when he wrote, "*Hear, O Israel: The LORD our God, The LORD is one.*"[48] And Malachi spoke of the significance of oneness in relating to God and a marriage partner when he declared: "*Has not the one God made you? You belong to him in body and spirit. And what does the one God seek? Godly offspring. So be on your guard, and do not be unfaithful*

---

[48] Deuteronomy 6:4

to the wife of your youth."[49] Faithfulness secures unity, a hallmark of truly intimate relationships.

Jesus beautifully explained the principle of oneness as He prayed for all believers:

> My prayer is not for them alone. I pray also for those who will believe in me through their message, that all of them may be one, Father, just as you are in me and I am in you. May they also be in us so that the world may believe that you have sent me. I have given them the glory that you gave me, that they may be one as we are one—I in them and you in me—so that they may be brought to complete unity.
>
> — John 17:20-23 —

The effectiveness seen in the ministry of Priscilla and Aquila was rooted in oneness with each other and with God, Himself. This kind of astonishing oneness is supernatural evidence that the Holy Spirit is consistently present at the center of the relationship. It is a sign that God has become the ultimate source of control and transformation within the marriage.

Supernatural oneness in marriage is characterized by the same unity of the Spirit and bond of peace spoken of by Paul. True peace cannot co-exist with any form of division. When even subtle discord creeps into a marriage relationship, both partners will sense the absence of this profound peace. God does not remove His peace to condemn us, but rather to make us aware that disunity is creeping in. Lapse of peace in a marriage relationship is a wonderful opportunity for spouses to discover the source of disharmony and refocus their attention on the pursuit of complete oneness.

---

[49] Malachi 2:15

Peace that passes understanding[50] is the direct result of the divine impartation of unity that comes through an intimate relationship with God. Our one God is the only source of true unity and peace. Aquila and Priscilla received these as gifts from God for their enjoyment and use in ministry. We, too, can experience this kind of abundance in life by pursuing oneness with God and accepting these astounding gifts. The purpose of pursuing oneness is so that we would all *"reach unity in the faith and in the knowledge of the Son of God and become mature, attaining to the whole measure of the fullness of Christ."*[51]

The story of Priscilla and Aquila portrays the beauty and effectiveness of co-heirs in Christ, co-laboring with one another in the glorious Kingdom of our God. Through their submission to each other and to Him, they fulfilled the purposes for which they were created, satisfying the destiny of true oneness in marriage. What they experienced and accomplished is just as possible today as it was in the first century. As it was in the beginning, so it shall always be—there are no limitations to the oneness and effectiveness of a marriage that is enveloped in the supernatural realm of God.

---

[50] See Philippians 4:7
[51] Ephesians 4:13

Chapter 4

Concluding Thoughts

_____

By Dr. Dan & Linda Wilson

N ATURAL VISION IS REALLY QUITE amazing. It involves two separate eyes constantly seeing similar, but different views of the surrounding world. Each eye sends electrical signals through over a million nerve fibers to the brain, where the conflicting data is processed, then recognized in our perception as a single, clear image.

Two eyes working together provide us with much better vision than a single eye on its own. Each eye gives the brain a different perspective of the world. When the two separate images are fused into one, we can see with clarity, true depth perception and a very wide field of view. The best possible vision occurs only when the two individual eyes quickly respond to signals from the brain so they are coordinated to perform with perfect synchronization.

Before Lasik[52] was FDA-approved in the United States, we traveled to Vancouver, Canada, to have our vision improved with

_____

[52] Laser-Assisted In-Situ Keratomileusis

laser vision correction. The results were completely remarkable. We were both given "monovision," in which the dominant eye is optimized for seeing at far distances, while the other is the best for seeing at near. The eyes alternately submit one to the other, depending on the distance to the object being viewed. When two eyes with monovision are coordinated by commands from the brain, everything that needs to be seen is clearly visualized with full appreciation of its shape, size and movement.

While writing this book, we realized that monovision could be seen as a parable of how co-heirs in Christ function together as one within marriage. Through his personality and gifting, Dan is generally the more dominant in our marriage relationship. Like the dominant distance eye in monovision, he focuses more on the big picture and has great clarity concerning the physical/spiritual environment in which we live. Dan sees God's far-off future plans as reachable goals that can be visualized in the present to remind us of where God is leading.

> Together, as one, we can perceive life with glorious clarity and exquisite detail.

Linda, on the other hand, functions more like the non-dominant eye that is best suited for seeing objects up close. She is amazingly gifted at recognizing practical things that need to be accomplished in the near future. The finest of details will not escape her focused observation, and her efforts to efficiently complete the task at hand are unrelenting.

Just as occurs with two eyes in monovision, we each observe life from a slightly different perspective, each focusing on the tasks God has placed before us in a somewhat unique way. At all times God individually leads us, yet His divine coordination enables the two of us to see and respond to life as if we were one. Nothing is too far away and nothing is too close. Together, as one, we can perceive life with glorious clarity and exquisite detail. This supernatural stereovision becomes possible when each of us willingly yields to God, allowing Him to have complete dominion over our marriage.

Through our thirty years of married life, we have learned the necessity of submitting all that we have and all that we are to God's control. Along the way, He has revealed to us the beauty and astounding potential of two individuals in submission to God, who also choose to submit to the desires, needs and gifts of their marriage partner. Obedience to Paul's command to *"submit to one another"*[53] is an essential step if we are to live as true co-heirs with Christ in marriage. Demonstrated on the cross as Jesus yielded to the will of the Father, appropriate submission is evidence of the presence of perfect love shared by two in an intimate relationship.

> Unity, peace and co-submission are the keys to releasing the full supernatural destiny of marriage.

In the Gospels, Jesus refers to the truth that two who are joined in marriage literally become *"one flesh."*[54] The astonishing oneness available to married believers is an extension of the supernatural oneness Jesus requested for us when He prayed that we *"may be one, Father, just as you are in me and I am in you."*[55]

We were married twenty-five years before asking God for this depth of marital oneness, because we didn't even know it

[53] Ephesians 5:21
[54] See Matthew 19:1-12 & Mark 10:1-12
[55] John 17:21

The flow of constant "little" submissions makes the need for either partner to submit in a "big" way quite rare.

existed! As co-heirs of God, we have received unity in the Spirit and have been blessed by an eternal bond of peace. Once a considerable challenge in our marriage, submitting to one another out of reverence for Christ has become a vital part of our relationship, cherished by us both. Unity, peace and co-submission are the keys to releasing the full supernatural destiny of marriage.

Inspired by the question of a young woman in Asia, it has been a joy to share our thoughts with you through writing the initial chapters of **CO- Powerful Partnerships in Marriage**. God has been pleased to share with us some of His wisdom concerning marriage, the most intimate of all relationships. He is prepared to do the same for all who long to know His truth. John tells the story of a man, blind from birth, who experienced the Truth and was miraculously healed.[56] It is our prayer that someday, like us, you and your spouse will joyfully echo his words, "One thing we do know: we were blind, but now we see!"

A Note from Linda

Submission is not a four-letter word. I'm sure this statement brings up many feelings within you: both positive and negative. I have often told Dan that it is easy to submit to a godly husband within a supernatural marriage. Many of you could wholeheartedly agree with me, as you also have experienced supernatural

---

[56] See John chapter 9

marriage; but others may not be blessed with a godly spouse. Whatever your case might be, I ask you to hear my heart as I describe a bit of our experience.

My teeth were horribly crooked in my childhood years. Admittedly, this might sound trivial to some, but its social impact on me was huge. I was ashamed to open my mouth, would speak only when necessary and would cover my mouth with my hand whenever I broke out with laughter. Thankfully, I had an excellent orthodontist—the transformation of my teeth was so great that he used my before and after pictures to show parents what he could do to help their child's teeth. Satan took this embarrassment, turned it into an ache in my heart and ran with it. As I matured, the insecurity grew in spite of my straightened teeth.

Meeting Dan was pivotal for me. He exuded confidence, making me feel safe when I was with him. He was kind, generous and loving. God used Dan to produce confidence and encouragement within me, often using him to challenge me and to push me out of my comfort zone in many arenas, especially socially. Dan leads by example. He is full of integrity and a man who fears the Lord.

Because of Dan's godly character, it is truly easy to submit to him; although I must confess at times it takes a moment or two for me to realize the wisdom of his way. Some years ago, I heard Richard Foster say that it is the easiest thing in the world to submit to God's will—except when it conflicts with yours. I think that is also true in mutual, godly submission between a husband and wife.

It is always better to be loving than to be right.

I propose that the need for submission going either direction—husband to wife or wife to husband—is continuous. The flow of constant, "little" submissions makes the need for either partner to submit in a "big" way quite rare. As we grow in honoring each other's strengths and become more graceful toward each other's weaknesses, the distribution of responsibilities becomes equitable. Both the man and the woman should feel appreciated for all they do to ease the flow of family life; also, both should freely give thanks and honor to the other for the part they play in bringing harmony and provision to the home.

At times, due to hectic schedules, illness, or whatever disruption might come, it is necessary to step up the role we play, occasionally assuming some of our spouse's responsibilities.[57] During those potentially stressful times, it is imperative to remain loving and kind. Our good friends, Paul and Teri Looney,[58] have taught us that it is *always* better to be loving than to be right.

---

[57] See the second chapter, "Proverbs 31: A Prophetic Model," for a discussion about occasionally assuming each other's responsibilities.
[58] Paul and Teri Looney have a chapter on page 67.

___Part Two___

___Present Powerful Partnerships___

Chapter 5

Submission & the Summit

By Dr. Paul & Teri Looney

WE DIDN'T MAKE IT ALL THE way to the top and it was my fault. The muscles in my arms were shaking with the strain of gripping the roll bar of the utility vehicle we had rented to traverse the trail to the summit of the 13,000-foot Hermit Peak in the Sangre de Cristo mountain range of southern Colorado. From all reports, a magnificent view awaited us, but my every breath came hard and I couldn't blame it all on the altitude. Paul piloted our little open vehicle as we climbed ever higher; from my vantage point of looking straight down the boulder-strewn mountainside, I felt vulnerable—unprotected.

Rewind fifteen years. This time Paul navigates our very large van along the twisting, icy road toward Wolf Creek in southern Colorado. Our destination is so close we can almost see the steam rising from the hot tub promised in the brochure. Paul is eager to arrive and is driving too fast on the icy roads. A patch of black ice, a slide into the oncoming traffic, a frantic correction and we skid off the road and down the mountainside, rolling over two and half times, landing upside down. Having been asleep in the back, I am tossed like a rag doll and go through the large rear window. You don't need all the gory details, but I sustained injuries that left significant physical and emotional scars.

So now, years later, Paul urges me to continue on with him to the top of Hermit Peak. He assures me our little vehicle can hold the road. He longs to reach the top but doesn't want to go on without me. I chicken out. We turn back.

Submission can be difficult—especially when you carry wounds from the past. Submission requires trust. Submission requires forgiveness. It requires humility and a decision to resist saying, "I told you so." Submission begs us to give up our anxieties and to let the peace of Christ reign in our hearts. With mutual submission, each encourages the other when facing obstacles that seem insurmountable. Not by accident, I think these hallmarks of submission echo the characteristics of love listed by the Apostle Paul in 1 Corinthians 13:4-8: Love is patient, love is kind. It does not envy, it does not boast, it is not proud. It is not rude, it is not self-seeking, it is not easily angered, it keeps no record of wrongs. Love does not delight in evil but rejoices with the truth. It always protects, always trusts, always hopes, always perseveres. Love never fails.

> Submission begs us to give up our anxieties and to let the peace of Christ reign in our hearts.

Back to my story: submission is difficult even after years of practice. I didn't do it perfectly this last trip to Colorado. While Paul thought that last steep stretch of road looked fun, I insisted we stop just a few hundred yards short. To me, it looked terrifying and my hands were already blistered from clinging to the roll bar.

Even so, my tenacity and deep breathing had already allowed me to realize one of my dreams. On the way up, I witnessed a magnificent black bear dashing down a hillside faster than I could ever imagine. Though we didn't make it to the summit, I was grateful to have spoken up and Paul was happy to honor my request.

I am a little sad that, at the last, my courage failed. I can see now that not trusting Paul with my life reflects a lack of trust in God. This is what God asks of us in Ephesians 5:22-24, "Wives, submit to your husbands as to the Lord. For the husband is the head of the wife as Christ is the head of the church, his body, of which he is the Savior. Now as the church submits to Christ, so also wives should submit to their husbands in everything." Ultimately, my life is always is God's hands.

My story is true, but it is also a parable of my life. Right now, today, I hear God calling me to the next level of submission in my journey with Paul. I hear Him calling me to submit even in my woundedness and fear. God calls me to surrender even with the knot in my stomach. He understands that sometimes I will be holding on to the roll bar with all my strength and He calls me to trust Him as my ultimate Protector.

> Submission, at its essence, is an act of profound, world-changing love.

Likewise, God challenges me to trust Him even when Paul does not love me perfectly. Sometimes he does veer off the road and I am injured as a result. It happens. We are imperfect. Only God's love is perfect.

Submission, at its essence, is an act of profound, world-changing love. In the past, I thought of submission as waving a white flag, saying, "Okay, okay! You win. I give up. You're right. You're always right. I'm always wrong." But that is not submission. That is capitulation. That is giving up and giving in. It sidesteps the hard work and heart work of true submission.

So what is true submission? In my gut, I recognize it and it is gut wrenching, "For God so loved the world that He gave His one and only Son that whoever believes in Him shall not perish but have eternal life." Do you see how God had to give His Son over to Satan, the prince of the world? He had to let go and give His Son for Satan to have his way with Him. How amazing that God's love prompted that degree of risk and surrender!

Jesus, too, wrestled with submission just before His crucifixion. He prayed, not once but three times, "My Father, if it is possible, may this cup be taken from Me. Yet *not as I will, but as You will*." After sweating great drops like blood, He chose His Father's will.

Father and Son both chose profound, world-changing love. They chose submission. The Father trusted the Son and the Son trusted His Father.

So how does this play out in marriage? How does it affect us as co-heirs with Christ? How do we choose this profound world-changing love?

First, be assured that in all things God asks of us, He is patient and kind. God knows there is a learning curve. He doesn't ask us to run before we learn to crawl. He does ask that we abide in Him day-by-day, making choices to love our spouse as He leads the way. Here are some practical suggestions:

- Pray together for wisdom and unity.

- Be quick to listen and slow to speak.

- Process your feelings with God before sharing them with your mate.

- Go there! Don't avoid conflict. It is an opportunity for

heart-felt sharing and mutual surrender. God wants peace-makers, not peacekeepers.

- Share from your heart. Use "I" statements (e.g. "I feel... I need... I wish... I hope... I believe...")

- Appeal to your partner for understanding, not agreement.

- Readily admit when you are wrong and when you cause pain to your mate; be quick to ask forgiveness.

- Learn to fight fairly and to resolve conflicts rather than rehearse them. Look ahead, not back.

- Avoid thinking "right-wrong" or "win-lose." We are partners!

- Dismantle your defenses rather than building a case. God wants lovers, not lawyers.

Love and trust increase with simple disciplines like these. Find a friend who encourages and supports you when you fail and challenges you to get up and go again. Remember to have patience, gentleness, kindness, forgiveness and protectiveness—all those qualities of love in 1 Corinthians 13—for yourself as well as your mate. Remember, you no longer live, but Christ lives in you (Galatians 2:20) and you certainly don't want to treat Him harshly!

Submission is an expression of honor and love. Ephesians 5 echoes Genesis 2:24, "'For this reason a man will leave his father and mother and be united to his wife, and the two will become one flesh.' This is a profound mystery—but I am talking about Christ and the church" (v. 31-33). As husbands and wives, we participate in this mystery. Just as Christ's loving submission to His Father changed the world, we are called to submit for love and change the world. It is a profound mystery and a profound privilege. It is ours.

Paul

For me, Paul, rolling the van those years ago was a horrifying wake-up call. It revealed, graphically, how vulnerable my family is to my decisions or lack of awareness. I did not make a conscious decision to put my family in harm's way, but pressing my agenda to reach our destination led to tremendous harm.

> Every wife needs to know her mate hears and honors her thoughts and feelings, her wishes and fears.

For me, the challenge is providing effective leadership while surrendering my own agenda. What a struggle it is to offer direction without being pushy or insisting on agreement. Many times, I try too hard to get Teri to see my point of view. Because I want her to agree with me, I say way too much and push way too hard, trying to get her to come around to how I see things.

Instead of making a humble request for what I want or need, I may make sideways hints, complain or adopt a "wait and see" attitude. Sometimes I justify and fortify my position. Instead of sharing my heart, I build my case. I am learning that I don't have to be right about my feelings or desires in order to have a right to those feelings and desires. Sharing them in a direct and loving way gives Teri opportunity to see me as I am and respond from her heart.

Likewise, when she shares with me, I am learning to reflect back with words that assure her I understand her heart in the matter. Every wife needs to know her mate hears and honors her thoughts and feelings, her wishes and fears. She needs to know he takes the matter to heart and will have conversations with

God and those he looks to for spiritual direction. It is not fair for me to ask submission from Teri if I am not practicing it myself.

When I set aside self-protection and speak openly and honestly, things go better. In many cases, unity flows easily and naturally from understanding and prayer. When it doesn't, God gives grace for me to "lay down my life" for Teri, or for her to yield to my desire. It was easy for me to turn back from Hermit Peak. I would rather be in the valley, communing with Teri, than alone on the summit. The hermit can have it!

As the old song says, "You've got to give a little, take a little and let your poor heart break a little. That's the story of, that's the glory of love." Mutual submission is a dynamic activity. A little like two children on a seesaw, husband and wife take turns deferring to one another. If our motive is love, we can enjoy the ride and take as much pleasure in yielding to our mate as we take in allowing him or her to accommodate us.

God has designed marriage to be challenging. Our personalities, perspectives and priorities are different, requiring that we give ourselves fully to love and accept one another as we are loved and accepted by God. Teri and I are learning to keep Him in the center. He is at work in everything for good and uses even our worst mistakes to bring us closer to Him and to each other. Even that nightmare roll in the van brought us closer.

God is committed to doing a work in us. He leads us toward a summit of love and unity. Our own goals and agendas pale in comparison to His great purpose—teaching us to love.

We can afford to be patient. So take a tip from our story; slow down and enjoy the ride. Trust me—you don't want to roll the van!

_____Chapter 6_____

When Three Become One

By Dr. Che & Sue Ahn

Husbands, live with your wives in an understanding way, as with a most delicate partner. Honor them as heirs with you of the gracious gift of life…

— 1 Peter 3:7, ISV —

ONE OF THE MOST IMPORTANT realities I have discovered about marriage is that two can never become one, only three can. What am I saying? A man and a woman can never truly become one, unless they each willingly and wholeheartedly submit to a third party—Jesus Christ. As each one freely puts himself or herself under obedience to the Lord, they will lovingly lay down their life for one another in mutual submission.

It sounds simple and straightforward enough on paper. However, I'm certain that every couple who struggles to become one has not only an odyssey to relate, but also view themselves as a work still in progress. I know this is true for my wife, Sue, and myself. I'd like to share a few high points in our journey that I trust will be helpful to you.

Off to a Good Start

In many ways, Sue and I had a great start in our marriage. We both had deep, personal commitments to the Lord and dedicated ourselves to obediently following Him as our primary priority in life. Although I lived for sex, drugs and rock-n-roll prior to my conversion at seventeen, as a new Christian, I immediately adopted sexual purity as a way of life. Sue and I had no difficulty agreeing to chastity before marriage and fidelity after. We carefully avoided situations while dating where we might be tempted to compromise and this helped to establish a strong bond of mutual trust between us.

> A man and woman can never truly become one, unless they each willingly and whole-heartedly submit to a third party – Jesus Christ.

We belonged to a conservative church planting movement that took marriage very seriously and required us to have nine months of premarital counseling. It may sound grueling, but actually it was very helpful as we were encouraged to share our views on every aspect of marriage. We also learned that marriage, as God intended it, was a covenant—an irrevocable commitment between husband and wife for life. Sue and I prayerfully made the decision that we would embrace our vows as a covenant and that divorce would not be an option. We have never deviated from that decision.

Other important decisions we made during our premarital counseling were to keep our romance alive by maintaining a date night each week and the importance of praying together daily. We also agreed that God's divine order for our life together was the Lord first, our marriage second, then our children and family, followed by ministry and career. We took all these decisions seriously—holding to them anchored us through some rocky times that were to come.

Adherence to Error

Along with the many benefits of our premarital counseling, we unfortunately inherited some error as well. Our conservative church held a very traditional, narrow view of the roles of husband and wife in marriage; namely the husband was the head and the wife was subordinate in everything, period. There was no place for women in ministry leadership. Sue and I accepted this worldview, as we had never been exposed to anything else.

We launched into marriage and family life as we welcomed our son, Gabriel, and three daughters, Grace, Joy and Mary. I was in full-time ministry and we were both very busy. Our marriage was slowly eroding, but I was oblivious. Outwardly, I was keeping all my premarital commitments. We had a weekly date night and I tried to do something special for Sue each week. We prayed together for the kids, had regular family devotions and a weekly family activity time. We even participated in a monthly marriage accountability group with other pastors.

For the first fifteen years of our marriage, we operated under the traditional, subordinate view of husband and wife we had been taught. We discussed things but final say was *mine*. I trusted my decisive, logical approach to problems over Sue's more intuitive, emotional view, which seemed mushy to me. My attitude was definitely, "I'm the boss applesauce." I was never physically abusive, but I was judgmental and critical of her input and frequently used Scripture as a weapon to remind her of her place and what her conduct should be like.

I was very performance oriented and confused my doing the right things with being the right husband for Sue. I didn't see how emotionally inaccessible I made myself. I was like a fortressed island, leaving Sue shut out from the deep, personal communication and bonding she longed for with me. Like a tiny rowboat, trying to find a safe haven on my island self, she kept meeting with resistance and rejection of her offerings of love and intimacy. She was a beautiful rose, fading for lack of life-sustaining water; emotionally dying right before me, but it didn't register on my logical radar.

> I was very performance oriented and confused my doing the right things with being the right husband...

Early Anchors Hold in the Storm

I knew our marriage wasn't perfect, but I actually thought we were doing well. Sue dutifully kept trying to cope with the status quo, but an internal storm was brewing and it erupted violently one summer's night in 1992. Sue had enough and angrily confronted me. Initially, I resorted to my righteous indignation and scriptural correction. She wasn't buying it. Instead, she emotionally withdrew, telling me she just couldn't stand any more hurt. I missed her warmth but decided to "wait it out," believing she would soon thaw. She didn't.

As weeks passed, I became more alarmed than angry. I tried gifts and asking for forgiveness—past effective strategies. The impasse remained. I finally had to admit this was different.

Something more basic had to change but I was clueless as to what it was. Fortunately, some of our early decisions served as powerful anchors during this dark, unsettling time that lasted the better part of four years.

We held to our covenantal vows and agreed that divorce was not an option. We could not run away and both had to face the fact that our marriage was in serious trouble. Although difficult, we held to our commitments of date nights, family devotions and activities and times of joint prayer. We admitted our current problems to our monthly marriage accountability group and asked the pastors there for prayer and support. We also sought marital counseling from a Christian professional. This was humbling for me, as I had to admit to myself that I was not such a competent "spiritual head" after all.

Laying the Axe to the Root

All these actions were helpful and things slowly began to improve. Sue and I were communicating in a more open and emotionally valid way. I began to understand and value more her emotional, intuitive input as I realized how it enriched our family life. I found myself listening more attentively when we discussed things and more frequently following her advice, which I often discovered was spot on.

But something was still hindering and it was in me, not Sue. I wanted to get to the bottom of it but didn't know how. In 1994, I attended a Toronto Revival meeting with an associate pastor. During the ministry time, while everyone around me was howling with joyful laughter, the Holy Spirit quietly did surgery in my soul. He brought up deep childhood wounds of rejection from my father and I wept profusely. He revealed an entrenched root of bitterness toward my father and my need to both confront and forgive him.

I began to understand that this bitterness was emotionally distancing me from everyone, especially Sue and my children. It took time, but when the opportunity presented itself during a visit from my parents, I was able to privately confront my father and ask for his forgiveness. He responded well and we had a powerful reconciliation. Laying the axe to this ancient root set me free emotionally for the first time in my life. With true heartfelt repentance, I asked Sue for forgiveness and we began rebuilding the trust in our relationship.

A Paradigm Shift

I was an emotional neophyte and increasingly, I began to value that Sue was an emotional pro. I stopped criticizing her intuitive gifts and began to appreciate them for the wise counsel they are. Advice I once had discounted as trivial, I now follow.

Sue is so much stronger in her EQ (Emotional Quotient) and relational skills than I am. She is the most powerful encourager I know. Like a life-giving river, she constantly encourages me, our children and everyone who crosses her path at our church. She tells me what birthday cards I need to write in my own hand and I submit to her every time—even though in my flesh, I do not see the importance of my handwriting or hers. But deep inside and from experience, I know she is right. She constantly teaches me that, in the emotional domain, small details convey a powerful message.

I'm so glad I've learned to defer often to her leadership in family matters. Sue's loving, giving heart nurtures us all. She is the key to our family loving Jesus and being so close. Although we are now empty nesters, Sue still holds everyone accountable to come together for a weekly family dinner night. These gathering times become all the more precious as our relationships continue to deepen and grow with our adult children. Most recently, we all rejoiced at the birth of our first grandchild, extending our family love to the next generation.

Becoming free emotionally allows me to communicate with more inner transparency to Sue, which brings us closer together. I understand her emotional heart better and have a strong desire to nurture and protect our relationship. My view of headship in my marriage has undergone a major paradigm shift. I no longer see Sue as a subordinate, but as my co-equal, sharing her strengths as we labor together as the senior pastors at our HRock Church in Pasadena, California.

I now realize that my role as head is to lead the way in providing servant leadership to Sue. By putting myself daily under the obedience of Christ, I have come to understand that next to loving Jesus, my most important commitment is to lay down my life in love for Sue. If I'm a failure in this commitment, I am a failure in life.

> It's His grace, not my willpower, that gives me the ability to lay down my life for Sue.

This has resulted in some major behavioral changes. I no longer make unilateral decisions. We agree that all expenditures over $500 are jointly made and for major decisions, we pray together until we reach agreement. We defer to each other's strengths, callings and words of wisdom. Our motto has become, "Being in right relationship is more important than being right."

The Fruit of Intimacy

I begin each day by asking the Holy Spirit to fill me afresh. I place myself, daily, under the obedience of Christ; for I know that only His love working in me can transform me into the servant leader He calls me to be. It's His grace, not my willpower, that gives me the ability to lay down my life for Sue. I focus on my heart and my actions, rather than monitoring hers. I find the more I lay down my life for her, the more she responds by laying down her life for me. Our intimacy has become a mutual self-amplifying process.

Marital intimacy yields glorious fruit! Together we are discovering that true marriage is a supernatural union between husband and wife in which two become one in body, soul and spirit through the consummating power of the Holy Spirit. It is the most vulnerable, personal, private form of sharing and bonding available to us here on earth. It requires the most attention and investment, but offers the safest place to receive healing, deliverance and be set free. When three become one, truly there is the restoration of the original seat of our God-delegated dominion and power.

Chapter 7

From the Back
to the Front

By Steve & Marci Fish

IMAGINE GOD AND ADAM IN THE garden. God looks at Adam and says, "It's not good for you to be alone, Adam; you need someone to serve you, work for you, someone you can boss around, someone who doesn't have any thoughts and ideas of her own, but is there to make your thoughts and ideas happen."

Sounds a little absurd to say it like that, but that seems to be the way some people look at the creation of Eve and consequently, the way they view marriage. In some places, an entire culture is built around this perspective of the relationship between men and women.

When God said, "It is not good for man to be alone," He was seeing man's need for intimacy and relationship. God, being three persons—Father, Son and Holy Spirit—is intimacy and relationship in Himself. Man was created for relationship with

God, but God saw that Adam needed someone more like himself to relate to, be intimate with and with whom to be fruitful and multiply. God wanted Adam to have the intimacy that He, Himself, embodies. He knew that Adam needed someone to share his life with.

For almost twenty-four years now, Marci and I have been sharing our lives together.

Supernaturally Arranged Marriage

One day while I was in seminary, my dad, who was a professor at the seminary, came to me and said, "Son, there is a girl in my 2:00pm class that I really want you to meet." He shared her name with me and I immediately went and looked her up in the student picture book.

"She looks great, Dad!" I said.

"Well Son, just because I'm getting older doesn't mean I've lost my eyesight," Dad jokingly replied.

I made a point to walk past my dad's 2:00pm class many times, hoping to catch a glimpse of Marci, but was always unable to meet her.

A few weeks later, Marci went up to my dad's office to turn in a book report.

"May I give my son your phone number?" he asked.

Marci had a great deal of respect for my dad, so she said, "Yes."

Shortly after this, I gathered up the courage and gave Marci a call. We went out on our first date... and we married several years later. Now, 23 years of marriage and 4 kids later, I'm very thankful for a dad who was able to spot the woman who was to be his son's wife.

The Couple that Prays Together...

Throughout the years, praying together has been one of the keys to walking together in unity in the Spirit. We prayed together so often in the early days of our relationship that it was actually in a prayer room where I asked Marci to marry me. I read her the prayer that I had written years earlier about what I desired in my future wife and said, "You are the answer to these prayers. Will you marry me?"

Amazing things happen when we pray alone; *incredibly* amazing things happen when we pray in agreement with someone else. That's why Jesus says:

> Again I say to you, that if two of you agree on earth about anything that they may ask, it shall be done for them by My Father who is in heaven.
>
> — Matthew 18:19, NASB —

I believe this is one of God's key plans for marriage. Marriage is an awesome opportunity for us to not only pray together, but to enter into a lifestyle of agreement prayer.

Revelation Keys

Another key to flowing in the supernatural in marriage has been revelation. One glimpse of heavenly perspective can change everything, and living a lifestyle of pursuing, receiving and acting on revelation from the Lord has been key in our marriage. We have learned that each revelation from the Lord is like a key that can unlock a new level of destiny. We have learned to value the small impressions and the major prophetic words that we have received.

In the early season of our marriage, Marci was content to minister in the background most of the time. She would pray, serve in the nursery and pour into our four amazing children. This was all great; however, she began to receive numerous prophetic words about a new season that she was going to transition into. The words began to come so often that it almost became predictable: "The Lord is moving you from the back, up to the front. You will teach and have a very powerful prophetic ministry. You and your children will travel the world, extending the Kingdom."

The beginning phase of this transition brought us into the most difficult season of our marriage. As Marci shares below, the Lord began to rebuild the very foundations of her life.

> **Praying together has been one of the keys to walking together in unity in the Spirit.**

During this time of intense spiritual battles, emotional struggles and sleepless nights, standing on the foundations we had laid in prayer, receiving revelation from God and holding on to that revelation were crucial to our survival.

I took recordings of Marci's key prophetic words and put them on my iPod. I listened to these words so many times that I actually memorized them. I prayed these words continually and at key times, I was able to encourage her by speaking them over her.

Stepping into the reality of these words required and continues to require radical change on both of our parts. This journey has now brought us into a season where we are learning to live and minister together as co-heirs. The Marci who used to be content hiding in the background is now a Marci who is up front, preaching and prophesying with me. The Marci who wanted to please everyone and would not confront anyone is now bold and definitely not afraid to confront. The Marci who hated to get on airplanes and wouldn't take risks is now a Marci who takes teams into remote African villages to preach the gospel with signs and wonders.

Marci's willingness to continually be transformed amazes me. Today, I'm so thankful to be living in the reality of the dream that I have always had of living and ministering in the Spirit together.

The Journey from Marci's View

There is a scene in the movie *The Princess Diaries* where Amelia finds out that she is a princess. In shock, she responds, "Shut up, shut up! You don't understand, I don't rule anything… my goal in life is to be invisible and I am good at it!" When this movie came out, I was in the middle of discovering who I really am and I so related to this scene. We are actually called to rule—all of us together—as co-heirs. I wanted to stay invisible, but I also wanted to reflect the image of God as I was created to do. So I was faced with a choice: step into who I am as a princess—as a co-heir—and rule with my husband, or remain in the back seat—invisible—and not take the place for which God created me. It was not an easy choice, but I can now say that being a princess for my King of kings and living with my prince as a co-heir has been one of the biggest and best choices I have ever made.

One glimpse of heavenly perspective can change everything…

Eight years ago, I began a journey to answer a question that I could no longer ignore: "Who am I really?" I came into marriage with a lot of personal insecurity and a lot of "ideals" about marriage—I wanted to be rescued and taken care of; I wanted to get into the back seat and let someone else drive; I wanted Steve to make the decisions. I wanted to coast. Steve was my knight in shining armor—loving, wise and very responsible. He gladly took over as my knight.

During our first two years of marriage, Steve finished seminary and I taught school—not many decisions to think about. During our third year of marriage, we had our first child and Steve began to pastor. We had four children in five years and a church that was growing from around 100 people to 700, so "coasting" is not a word I would use to describe those years. During this season, I still managed to remain relatively hidden and in the back seat but I was also beginning to unravel. My insecurities were surfacing to the point of causing high-level anxiety in me. My goal in life during these first years of marriage, parenting and pastoring, was to make sure everyone was happy. This is the way I approached pretty much everything and I wanted Steve to do the same—make everyone happy. With four children and a church of 700 people, the mere thought of having the responsibility of everyone's happiness is enough to make you shudder.

By the fall of 2002, I was losing it and by January of 2003, I felt everything crashing in. I was depressed, not eating, not sleeping and barely able to function in the basics of everyday life. I looked forward to putting the kids to bed at night so I could sit with Steve and cry. It was the best of times and the worst of times. This "undoing" was the very thing that I needed to become the person that God created me to be and to truly find myself. During that time, God told me that I wanted to give my life away but I didn't have it to give. I wasn't really a "help meet" to my husband, because I was really just existing and not participating. I thought that humility meant laying all of my thoughts and feelings aside to honor my husband, my children, my friends and my church. I kept getting prophetic words from people that said, "God says that if you will take your place, you will free others to take their place." I didn't understand these words because I thought that in order for others to take their place, I had to get out of the way.

It has been a journey that, though painful at times, has been completely wonderful and worth every tear and every difficult step. I have discovered that God was right and my becoming who I am and taking my place has brought new freedom to those around me, including my husband. Instead of running behind Steve, sometimes dragging my feet, I now run beside him. I can actually help Steve in greater ways now that I engage in the decision-making and share how I see and feel about things. Steve is not left with all of the pressure and responsibility of everything; I am there with him. This is actually more helpful than staying behind or off the track somewhere, trying to influence in unhealthy ways. There are always times when it feels like it would be easier to just do things the way you want, or the way you think is best, without letting anyone else get involved, but we have found that the benefits of

> "God says that if you will take your place, you will free others to take their place."

doing things together far outweigh the benefits of "easiness." We have also found that praying together is not optional. We must endeavor *together* to find out what God is doing and get in on His plan. Ultimately, it is not my plan or Steve's plan that we are after; it is God's plan. His ways and His thoughts are so much higher, greater and absolutely worth pursuing together. We are co-heirs, which means that we have an inheritance. That is our passion and our pursuit together: to live in our inheritance as a son and a daughter of the King of kings; to live in His presence together and to be a manifestation of Him on the earth. It is not really Steve's way or my way, but rather *God's* way. We need each other and we are so thankful that we get to be on this journey together.

Steve is my hero and has been, for me, the embodiment of unconditional love. He made room for me and encouraged me to come into my place next to him. He has cheered me on and pulled me up. The journey has not been without challenges, "courageous conversations," and mistakes, but the view from the front seat is spectacular! We are navigating life together. Our strengths help each other's weaknesses and our perspectives are much greater together.

> Though one may be overpowered by another, two can withstand him. And a threefold cord is not quickly broken.
>
> — Ecclesiastes 4:12, NASB —

Chapter 8

Together:
From Vegas to Igloo

By Joshua & Janet Angela Mills

The LORD directs the steps of the godly. He delights in every detail of their lives.
— Psalm 37:23 —

AFTER MAKING IT THROUGH AN ICY snowstorm, a dangerous car accident, receiving angelic protection, a supernatural financial miracle and a divine airplane delay, we finally arrived in Puvirnituq, Nunavik, somewhere in the Eastern Canadian Arctic. This place was like nothing else we had ever experienced in our lives. It was six o'clock in the morning and sixty-five degrees below zero outside. Our bodies shivered in ways we had never experienced before—we were human popsicles stuck inside an Arctic freezer. There was no way for us to leave, because our igloo had been tightly sealed shut with packed snow and the saw we needed to cut through the ice was sitting on the outside of our frozen hut. Even if we did manage to get out, there was no one close to help us.

> Do not despise these small beginnings, for the LORD rejoices to see the work begin...

We had arrived hours earlier to a warm Inuit greeting of tea and cookies. A man named Adame, the championship Igloo builder in town, had prepared this special home for us to stay overnight. Several of his friends welcomed us inside the toasty igloo that had a fire burning to keep things warm. We removed our winter coats and boots, laid them on the icy floor and enjoyed the company of our precious Inuit friends. After they said goodbye and left us alone for the night, our eyes began to burn because of the gases being released from the camping stove within our close quarters. We decided to turn off the flame and go to sleep for the night. Now, in the wee hours of the morning, we were writhing with indescribable pain as the cold temperature penetrated our bodies.

After we attempted to start a fire and accidentally ignited the rope of our sleeping bag on fire instead, we decided the best thing to do was to just hold on to each other for dear life and allow our body temperatures to keep us warm as we snuggled in our little winter home. At this point, it was quite obvious to us that we wouldn't make very good Inuits... but one thing we knew for sure—with Jesus in the middle of it all, we would get through this situation, no matter what. This is the way our relationship began and it has always remained that way; Jesus Christ has been the center of our marriage. I want Janet Angela to go back to the beginning and tell you how it all started...

Supernatural Beginnings

Do not despise these small beginnings, for the
LORD rejoices to see the work begin …

— Zechariah 4:10, NLT —

Joshua and I were both born and raised in loving Christian families with wonderful parents who have set godly examples in our lives. We will always be thankful for the relationship they had with each other and with us.

In my teenage years, I determined in my heart to wait for the man that God had for me and that I would enter into a relationship with him only upon the direction of the Holy Ghost. My heart's desire was to serve God wholeheartedly and place Him first in my life before anyone or anything else.

When I was 19 years old, God placed that young man in my life. I attended a small church in my hometown of Leamington, Ontario, Canada; we had an amazing youth group where I developed a great friendship with Joshua Mills. He was a praise and worship leader in our church and also a part of the youth group. When Joshua began to pursue me, I asked the Lord if Joshua was really "the one"—I only wanted the person that God intended for me. One beautiful thing about God is that He wants to meet our heart's desire too.

Take delight in the LORD, and he will give you
your heart's desires.

— Psalm 37:4, NLT —

After several months, I knew that, indeed, Joshua was the *right* one. From the beginning, it was so sweet and innocent—we both had to work up the nerve to hold each other's hand. Joshua was my first and only boyfriend and I am so happy to say that I love him more each and every day.

As soon as we decided to get into a more serious relationship, Joshua had to move back to his hometown of London, Ontario, Canada, which was two hours away. This began our long distance relationship. The distance continued to grow over the next several months—God promoted Joshua in his ministry and he eventually moved to Florida and then on to California. Through all the transitions, we knew that we had to put God first in our relationship. We trusted the Lord in this.

On September 7th, 1999, I flew to San Diego, California, for seven days, where Joshua was living at the time. We hadn't seen each other for almost seven months but as soon as we saw one another at the airport, it was like there was no distance or time between us. We had a wonderful week full of sightseeing and adventurous day trips. Joshua was so sweet—he had designated a budget for each day and had planned everything we would do, including going to the beach, the zoo and Disneyland.

On Sunday afternoon, as we were driving to church, Joshua suggested we drive to Las Vegas to see all the lights along the famous strip. So after the service, we made the six-hour drive to Las Vegas. We cruised down the Boulevard and admired the dazzling lights and night-time spectacle of the Las Vegas skyline. We had never seen anything quite like this in our entire lives!

We stopped for dinner and as we finished eating, we noticed a little wedding chapel just across the street. We ran across the road and as a joke, we had a complete stranger take our picture in front of the chapel. We got back in the car and drove all the way back to San Diego. The next day, after a few hours of sleep, we went to Tijuana, Mexico, for a day of shopping. It was there, in Tijuana, that Joshua looked at me and asked me to drive back to

Las Vegas with him so that we could get married that night. I was shocked! I wanted to marry him... but that night? Within a few hours...? There was so much to think and pray about that my response was, "No." I shared with him how much I wanted to be his wife but that I didn't think I could do it that night. I had a lot to consider – I had family, church, ministry and job responsibilities. But Joshua was very determined and kept asking me throughout the day if I would marry him that night.

Later that evening, we went with Joshua's pastors to Qualcom Stadium for a San Diego Padre's baseball game. During the game, Joshua looked at me and quietly asked, "Will you marry me tonight?" Immediately, I felt the peace of God and I replied with a resounding "YES!" As soon as I said that word, the famous Dixie-Cups song, *Going to the chapel and we're going to get maaaaarried* played over the loud speakers throughout the stadiums. No one had heard or knew what we were discussing—this was a supernatural sign and confirmation to us.

We then shared with the Pastors that we were going to drive to Las Vegas and get married that night. Joshua's pastors were both excited because earlier in the week, they had individually received a word from the Lord that Joshua and I would be married before the end of the week. They wrote it down in their Bibles and didn't discuss it with each other, or with us. They didn't want to influence a decision; they knew that if it was the Lord, it would happen. They sent us off with a blessing and we began our drive back to Las Vegas late into the night.

It was very early morning when we began driving from chapel to chapel, looking for a place where we could be married. We finally pulled into the *Little White Chapel Tunnel of Love* drive-thru wedding chapel and ordered the most affordable option on the menu board. We pulled through the drive-thru and the pastor and witness met us outside. It was there, surrounded by the little painted cherub angels in the tunnel, that we made our vows and became one in marriage. It was so beautiful. We knew that God was watching us and that He had placed us together for His purposes.

A few weeks later, we had a beautiful ceremony in Canada with our friends and family to celebrate our marriage. I then moved to San Diego to start our life together as husband and wife. We didn't know how everything was going to work out, but we knew we had Jesus and each other. As long as you have Jesus Christ in the center of your marriage, everything will be great. I will let Joshua explain this a little further…

See the Treasure in Each Other

In our marriage we have learned how important it is to encourage one another. It's essential to see the treasure that God has placed within your spouse. Instead of focusing on negatives, look for the positive things that cause you to flourish together. It is vital to communicate positive, uplifting words to your spouse. Every day, we tell one another how much we love each other and how thankful we are for one another. Some of our spiritual mentors told us that when they wake up in the morning, they kiss each other 100 times before getting out of bed. What a great idea! Purposefully beginning every day together in love. We pray together and always share our genuine feelings and thoughts. Someone once said, "The couple that prays together, stays together."

> Instead of focusing on negatives, look for the positive things that cause you to flourish together.

Janet Angela and I have also learned how to listen to each other's dreams, visions, goals and ideas. There is so much revelation that flows in our lives as we continually submit ourselves to the Holy Spirit. We support one another in what God shows us to do and we work together toward its accomplishment.

People have told us that they don't know how they could ever work with their spouse, as they need the time apart or they would be driven crazy. We can honestly say that we are only crazy in love. We love spending every minute of every day with each other. We are husband and wife, passionate lovers, ministry partners and best friends. We are one.

We have learned how we flow together, especially when it comes to flowing in ministry. Bringing our different giftings together has made us complete and allowed us to have a more dynamic ministry. We appreciate the differences in each other and the unique anointing that God has given to each of us. *As we find ourselves in Christ, we discover our full potential together.*

- Do you desire to have a loving relationship—filled with companionship, tenderness, kindness and overflowing generosity toward one another?

- Do you dream about a protective and safe marriage that allows you to share your deepest concerns and yet discover the greatest peace you've ever known?

- Do you want to experience sex so fulfilling that you are in a blissful state of satisfaction all the time?

- Do you wish that you could have perfectly clear communication with your spouse?

I have discovered the answer for these things within the pages of the Bible…

One of my favorite Scriptures is Psalm 133—it is an absolutely beautiful representation of what God can do with anyone who desires to walk in the unity of the Spirit. This includes marriages.

> How good and pleasant it is when brothers live together in unity! It is like precious oil poured on the head, running down on the beard, running down on Aaron's beard, down upon the collar of his robes. It is as if the dew of Hermon were falling on Mount Zion. For there the LORD bestows his blessing, even life forevermore.
>
> — Psalm 133:1-3 —

Where there is unity, God releases His supernatural oil—healing, prosperity and blessing. Did you notice that this oil flows from the head down? It never flows from the feet upward. As we are submitted to the Lord, He causes our marriage relationships to be filled with overflowing blessings. The morning dew also comes in that place of unifying glory. The dew is what causes us to grow and flourish in our God-given abilities! I am going to let Janet Angela show you this...

Unity Through Priority

> Do two walk together unless they have agreed to do so?
>
> — Amos 3:3 —

God loves divine order. We have discovered a divine order that works successfully in our family and marriage. First and foremost, God is our number one priority. Through our intimate relationship with Christ flows everything we need and want. In this realm of intimacy is supernatural provision, heavenly revelation, wisdom to make decisions, and guidance. When we put God first, everything else follows in rightful succession.

Secondly, we have placed each other and our immediate family. We love each other dearly and we love our wonderful son, Lincoln, and our new baby daughter, Liberty. We love to talk, to have fun, to laugh and we love to enjoy each other's company. It is so healthy to have supernatural joy in your marriage, it is an absolute priority. We know how to work really hard, but we also know how to play hard… and this keeps things in balance.

> Jesus Christ, the hope of glory, resides in us individually, in our marriage, in our family and in our ministry.

Thirdly, we have placed our ministry, friends and other relationships. Our marriage and family is healthy and happy as we have chosen to live in this order. Everything flows from the top downward. When your priorities are set straight, you will have divine unity.

We recognize the glory in our lives and give the Lord thanks and praise for what He has divinely placed together. Jesus Christ, the hope of glory, resides in us individually, in our marriage, in our family and in our ministry.

Discovered Together!

With our winter coats and boots spread across the igloo floor, we continued to hold on to each other tightly, knowing that we could make it through our icy stay as long as we stuck together. We prayed in tongues for what seemed to be an eternity and worshiped the Lord in that frigid Arctic air. Thinking back on that time now, it was such a beautiful moment—just being together and being thankful for each other; recognizing that our lives depended on each other and on God. Finally, after a couple of hours, we began to hear the squeaking sound of a saw cutting through the igloo dome. Our friends had returned to take us to their homes for breakfast. We quickly welcomed their warm blankets and parkas and rushed onto their snowmobiles for a ride back into town. Now, eight years and forty nations later, we will still never forget the time we spent with each other in the igloo!

Chapter 9

Loved, Valued & Fulfilled

By Bart & Kim Hadaway

HELLO, WE ARE BART AND KIM Hadaway. We have had the privilege of enjoying 31 years of marriage and have been blessed with three wonderful children and seven amazing grandchildren. Through our life together, we have learned valuable lessons in how to maintain and grow our relationship. We believe that, for the most part, we have experienced what God intended marriage to be before the fall of man in the Garden of Eden. But, because we do live in this fallen world and have the propensity for sin that exists in all of us, we have also experienced the trials and challenges of marriage. Through the finished work of the cross, we are continually in the process of becoming one with Him—and each other. We would like to share how we have learned to celebrate each other in all of our strengths and how to empower one another in areas of weakness.

Bart

The most important lesson Kim and I learned was the necessity of finding our value in our individual relationships with God. We were not serving God when we first married, so we sought fulfillment in our marriage *without* Him. But as we turned our hearts to the Lord, we soon discovered that any attempt to find our value apart from the revelation of His love for us as individuals caused us to place impossible demands upon each other. Colossians 2:10 says that we are complete in *Him* (Christ Jesus). In every human heart, there is a place that only God can satisfy. When we find our identity and value in Him alone, it prepares us to love and serve our mates instead of demanding that they serve and satisfy us. It's a Kingdom principle that the more we give, the more we receive. So, the more whole and secure we become in Christ, the more freedom we experience to serve and enrich the lives of our mates. The more we live to serve our spouse, the more we enjoy the blessings of marriage as God intended—spiritually, emotionally and physically.

> When we find our identity and value in Him alone, it prepares us to love and serve our mates instead of demanding that they serve and satisfy us.

Kim

As far back as I can remember, I desired to have a husband and children. I dreamed of my husband, as I believe many women and young girls do. In Proverbs 18:22, Scripture states that he who finds a wife finds a good thing. I know the same is true of a godly husband and I am here to say that I have not been disappointed!

As my husband stated, when we met we were not serving the Lord, so we tried to find complete fulfillment in each other. Man cannot bring total fulfillment; this is something only God can do. But I did experience being fulfilled and healed through God's love combined with the love of a godly husband.

One example of this happened many years ago, when Bart and I, along with our three children, had just moved to a new community. We had traveled a long distance, separated by miles from family and friends, to pastor a church. Bart and I had been on a blessed eleven-year journey with the Lord, but we realized that we were just beginning.

> ...My value and worth has nothing to do with what I do but rather, who I am as a daughter of God.

We have always had great communication in our friendship and marriage (a *must* for a healthy marriage); but while beginning this chapter in our lives, we hit a bump. Actually, I hit a bump and Bart got to take the ride with me. Areas of weakness in my life began to manifest on a grand scale. I went on a roller coaster ride of depression, rooted in rejection, that lasted eighteen months. I was able to hide it from most everyone, but I could not hide it from my husband—he knew me too well.

A place of security was pulled out from under me and I had to discover that my husband was not my source. I realized that I would throw prayers up to God and then run to Bart to meet the need. I felt I had little worth or value and I hit a point where I battled thoughts of death and hopelessness. I believed that my husband and children needed someone who had it all together, and that wasn't me. In my mind I had the world's concept of what a good wife and mother was supposed to look like and I did not measure up.

Why am I sharing this story? Because God broke through and pierced me with His great Love! He just happened to use my amazing husband in this process. Bart was always there to point me to Father God and hear my heart and my pain. He diligently prayed *for* me and *with* me for victory, while he encouraged and cheered me on. Bart constantly reminded me that my value and worth has nothing to do with what I do but rather, *who I am* as a daughter of God.

Communication, trust, submission and complete vulnerability were so valuable in this process. Had Bart and I not had good communication or trust established in our relationship, I would have been a sinking ship. I give God praise for every bit of this.

> ...In marriage as one flesh, Adam and Eve were an expression of the unity of the Godhead.

Early in our marriage, we had established trust and safety in our communication. While it is imperative that we trust our mates, trust must go to an even deeper level. It must be a trust that is founded upon God *in* them. In other words, while our mates will never be perfect, we can trust God to always be at work in them (Philippians 2:13 & Hebrews 13:21). This prevents us from setting ourselves up with unreal expectations and disappointment. It also allows us to be honest, open and vulnerable in our weaknesses and struggles.

Bart
Valuing Kim

Eve was not created as an afterthought, "made from a rib, a cheaper cut." Though Eve was not mentioned until chapter two of Genesis, from the beginning God created mankind, male and female (Genesis 1:26-27). Just as Jesus was the "express image of the invisible God" (Hebrews 1:3), Adam and Eve were created to be a representation of the image of God in the earth. Individually, they were created as an expression of the very being and nature of God. But in marriage as one flesh, they were an expression of the unity of the Godhead.

Several years ago, when we were pastors of a church in the Midwest, I invited a prophetic minister to come and speak to our church. While I knew the man from being one of my instructors in the ministry school I had attended, he did not know me personally. But he began to speak into my life almost as soon as we started the two-hour drive home. He showed me that I did not value my wife as I should, pointing out specific areas where I placed value upon Kim as my wife and what she could do for me as my wife, instead of valuing her *first* as a daughter of God. He shared details that could have only been revealed to Him by God. I responded in all the "proper" ways externally, but—I have to be honest—I was angry on the inside. It did not feel good! I took it all to the Lord in prayer and He began to confirm what I already knew in my heart—all that the man said was true. To this day, I am thankful for his boldness. I know it was done in love.

I approached Kim and shared what had happened. I asked her to forgive me and help me be a better husband. I told her I wanted to value her as a daughter of God first and secondly, as my wife. The wonderful thing is that I knew I could trust Kim.

As she previously stated, this kind of trust must be established to allow us to be vulnerable with one another. Through processes like these, we are able to validate and encourage each other in our areas of strengths and weaknesses.

Bart & Kim

We want to share a very short version of how God graced us to be able to help and strengthen each other in one of the most trying times of our lives. Our oldest daughter became rebellious in her early teen years. This led to her being a prodigal for over eight years. There were many times when we would think things could not get any worse, but they did. During this period, we both went through times of extreme discouragement. Consequently, we did not always respond to our daughter as we should have. There were many times when one of us would be full of faith and the other would be full of weariness and vice versa. Often, the battle was so intense that we each experienced feelings of giving up, but we also experienced the benefit of being strengthened by one another. When Bart would be very angry or feel like giving up, Kim would be an unmovable rock. At other times, Bart would be able to encourage and speak faith and hope into Kim.

As we learned to grow in absolute faith, trust and dependence upon God, we also discovered how God had given us each other to grow as one in Him. Too often, in our trials of life, the enemy is able to bring separation between husbands and wives. We want to encourage you that these are also the times that you have the opportunity to grow not only closer to God, but also to each other. By the grace of God, we were able to become united to the point that our intercession and warfare strategy against the enemy was multiplied. Surely, one can put a thousand to flight and two can put ten thousand to flight! Today, our daughter is the most amazing young woman of God. We can truly say that everything the enemy meant for harm, God turned for good. He always has the last word!

We want to leave you with one final word of exhortation and encouragement; we have found this truth to be one of the most beneficial aspects of our marriage during the good and the bad times:

DON'T FORGET TO LAUGH!

Chapter 10

For Better or Worse

By Robert & Katie Souza

For I know the thoughts that I think toward you, saith the LORD, thoughts of peace, and not of evil, to give you an expected end.

— Jeremiah 29:11, KJV —

Beginnings

IT WAS ONLY IN THE LAST NINE years of my incarceration that I (Robert) lived as a Christian. During that time, I spent nearly every awakened moment consuming the Scriptures or some other related material. I had no idea for what the Lord was preparing me, though time would soon tell that it was more than I ever imagined.

In March of 2003, I was released from prison. They transferred me to what is called a "halfway" house. It was a co-ed facility, which allowed inmates to begin the process of reintegration with society. Each week they held various group meetings with attendance being mandatory for all. It was here that the Lord first introduced me to the woman who would soon become my wife. I never wavered in this revelation; however, there was one small problem—I discovered that convincing my soon-to-be bride of this same truth would become a great challenge!

Katie had also just been released from prison. From the initial day of our meeting, it seemed like all she could talk about was her purpose and ministry vision. I recall the first time I even hinted at our being together, she looked me straight in the face and without hesitation said, "I can't get married, I'm on a mission from God!" You can imagine her surprise when, only days later, I began pressing the matter further. I would call her and say things like: "Good morning, Mrs. Souza. How are you today?" or "Hello Mrs. Souza, this is your husband." At first she refused to take me seriously, responding in ways like, "Keep on dreaming" and "Good luck with that!" But persistence ran its course and eventually Katie came to the realization that I, too, was on a mission from God—and she was it!

The day finally arrived when Katie said that unless she, too, received a direct Word from the Lord, not only would there be no wedding bells, but all further communication with us would cease! To which I simply replied, "You will get confirmation. It is coming and it is coming soon!" She then said, "Ha, we'll see about that!" A week later, just as I prophesied, God did visit Katie, saying, "You have a message in your heart for Robert." When she asked what that message was, the Lord *directly* told her, "I do!" On April 16, 2004, we were indeed pronounced husband and wife!

In the summer of 2005, I began to have many thoughts about starting my own business. One night while I prayed and sought the Lord for direction, I received the Word: "I will increase your business so that she (Katie) can be about My business." It would be a total step in faith that would undoubtedly take us outside our comfort zone. We were ready, believing for a miracle and a miracle is precisely what came next! Within the first three months, we earned more than we did the entire previous year. By the end of the first year, my new company had already become a multi-million-dollar corporation.

The business began fully supporting Expected End Ministries, enabling Katie to be about the "Father's business" full-time. She had also completed the writing of her book, *The Captivity Series: The Key to Your Expected End.* We were able to publish and distribute tens of thousands of free copies into prisons all over the world. It was an amazing and fulfilling time! There we were, two crowns of God's mercy and grace, living and working together, advancing the Kingdom of Heaven!

Now the serpent was more cunning than any beast of the field which the Lord God had made.

— Genesis 3:1, NKJV —

Trials

How solemn a time it must have been for Adam and Eve to look back on that awful and dreadful day of their fall. As the prodigal son would later cry out, "Father, I have sinned against heaven, and in thy sight, and am no more worthy to be called thy son" (Luke 15:21, KJV). Most assuredly, none would have ever imagined such a heart-wrenching departure from their loving God. In like manner, if someone had told me of the coming day when I, too, would be taken captive by the snare of the devil to do his will (2 Timothy 2:26), I would have denied it twice over.

And yet, that is exactly what happened. In this limited space, I cannot give a full account of all that took place, though I do wish to be transparent.

While in prison, I was diagnosed with severe bipolar disorder. I had experienced terrible mood swings accompanied by obsessive and compulsive behavior. It was actually this diagnosis that first led to my understanding of the many previous years of alcohol and drug abuse. In essence, I lived with an imbalance in my system and continually self-medicated to reduce the endless anxieties I constantly felt. At one point during my incarceration, I honestly believed that a healing had taken place. However, through the course of time, I began to experience the same symptoms riddling me all over again. I went to a doctor a few years after my release and started taking prescription medications. This led to my defenses being lowered and not long after, I began drinking. From that point on, everything spiraled downward. It progressed until I finally picked up another old habit—I became addicted once more to heroin.

All the blessings bestowed upon us, everything we worked so hard to achieve, the hope and promise that was ours—now in jeopardy of being lost. Life became a living nightmare with Katie experiencing the deepest blow of all. There came a point when she could bear the abuse no longer and returned to live with her mom and dad. At the time, I was completely out of control. On three different occasions I was rushed to the emergency room in an overdosed state. There was no mistake, I was clearly marked for death. As I live and breathe today, it is an undeniable miracle of God that I survived. I attempted

> I realized how my sin had become a catalyst to lead my wife into sin.

numerous things to break the cycle, including counseling and multiple in-patient clinics—all to no avail. At one stage, Katie tried moving back home, making every effort to help and care for me. Even when that failed, she interceded with much prayer and fasting. Toward the end, I spent nearly every waking moment in sickness and withdrawals. I had given up and lost all hope of recovery. I didn't know what more to do.

Then it happened—I received a call from Katie. She told me how she could not bear the burden much longer; I had abandoned her and she had been fighting for my return for a long time. Then, in the middle of our crisis, her mom died a horrible, painful death. Katie was totally broken. With all that transpired, the heartache and misery had caused a door to be opened by the enemy. She was being tempted to fall into the arms of another man. Nothing had yet occurred, but she was very fearful and confused.

> **I cried out to God like never before... What had seemed impossible, suddenly became attainable.**

Upon hearing this, it was as if my mind and emotions exploded. My whole life seemed to flash before my eyes. In that moment, for the very first time, I realized how my sin had become the catalyst to lead my wife into sin. I could hear the words of Jesus:

> And if anyone causes one of these little ones who believe in me to sin, it would be better for him to be thrown into the sea with a large millstone tied around his neck.
>
> — Mark 9:42 —

What had I done?! It was this solemn thought that drove me to my knees. I cried out to God like never before. I begged for His mercy and strength. What had seemed so impossible, suddenly became attainable. From that moment on, I never touched another drink or drug again. Within weeks, Katie and I were back together and we began our life all over again. We came through a horrific experience and discovered that through it all, God made a way to bring us closer together than ever before. To this day, we stand in awe at how Jesus worked all things out for His Glory and our good (Romans 8:28).

> Keep your lives free from the love of money and be content with what you have, because God has said, "Never will I leave you; never will I forsake you."
>
> — Hebrews 13:5 —

Obedience

In 2008, the economy crashed and my business came to a screeching halt. Suddenly, we were completely out of work. I began to collect unemployment while Katie worked for the ministry without pay. We assessed all of our expenses and cut back wherever we could. We were getting by but with very little to spare. I was growing ever more concerned for what the future held. It was during this time of drought and doubt that I made a dangerous decision—I began withholding our tithe. Months went by and then one night, while trying to sleep, I suddenly felt what could only be described as the deep dread of God. I dozed off again only to awaken once more to the same feeling. I immediately understood what it was: I had sinned by robbing the

Lord and could now see the cause of our personal lack. This sent me into a panic. I was driven out of bed and in the middle of the night, I wrote an offering check for $2,000. It was everything we had left.

The next morning, I explained to Katie all that occurred. She looked at me in amazement and proceeded to tell me how she also received a Word from the Lord on the very same thing, just days earlier. Since that time, she had been in deep repentance, prayer and warfare. It was such a confirmation and relief that we were on the right track. A week later, I received a call from a prior customer. Nearly a year earlier, our company had submitted a proposal to them for a remodeling project. They were contacting me to inform us that they were getting ready to finally start the construction and that our bid was accepted. When I hung up, I immediately remembered the tithe. The whole job took less than three weeks to complete and at the end of it, we made a profit of $80,000. We certainly learned our lesson and made sure we gave the Lord His portion out of it. Six months later, the same company contacted us again. This time we finished the job in less than six weeks and earned another $250,000. We never again questioned the Lord's providence over our lives. Once more we survived and made it through together.

> **What the Lord begins, He always completes.**

> And the two will become one flesh. So they are no longer two, but one.
> — Mark 10:8 —

Purpose

In the middle of 2009, the ministry exploded. Suddenly there were countless matters needing attention. It was then that Katie lost her head administrator. There was no way Katie could continue in her travels from state to state, holding conferences and visiting prisons, without someone overseeing the planning of events, office management, shipping out resources and keeping the accounting accurate.

Suddenly, the Lord called me. I realized that all those years of studying and training were in preparation for such a time as this! I signed my company over to my business partner and committed all of my time to the ministry; soon I was appointed Director of Operations. I look back on how far we have come—we continue to have our trials as we are getting our souls healed, but we always keep one revelation in the forefront of our minds: *What the Lord begins, He always completes* (Philippians 1:6).

About the Authors

Powerful CO-heirs in Ministry

Dr. Dan & Linda Wilson

Believing that supernatural marriages are a sign and a wonder in the world today, Dr. Dan and Linda Wilson have dedicated their lives to drawing couples into this Holy Spirit-driven type of intimacy. Happily married for 30 years, Dan and Linda are the co-founders of Supernatural Marriage Ministries in Fort Worth, Texas.

They love being "Grandma Lindy" and "Papa D" to three precious grandchildren. Dan has authored **Supernatural Marriage** and its study guide **Experiencing Supernatural Marriage**. Sharing revelation through conferences, television, radio and books, the Wilsons cast a vision of hope to the nations that every marriage can be blessed through the love, wisdom and transforming power of God.

Dr. Paul & Teri Looney

Dr. Paul and Teri Looney live a bit north of Houston, Texas. Paul practices psychiatry while also on staff as a pastor at Woodlands Church. In addition, he is the director of Hidden Manna Ministries. Paul and Teri conduct the "One Flesh" retreat for couples as well as other workshops. They have a passion for sharing what they have learned about the challenges and rewards of marriage.

They married in 1983 and their sons, Adam, Joel and Jon Paul bring them great strength. Daughter-in-law, Krissi, brings them beauty and granddaughter, Rin, brings Sunshine.

Steve & Marci Fish

Steve and Marci Fish have a passion for the presence of the Lord. They love to lead individuals and churches into life-changing encounters with God. They carry an apostolic anointing and enjoy working with leaders locally and internationally, bringing practical revelation and powerful impartation for kingdom advancement.

Steve and Marci are senior leaders at Convergence Church in Fort Worth, Texas, where they have served for 21 years. They are parents of four wonderful children.

Dr. Che & Sue Ahn

Dr. Che Ahn and his wife, Sue, are founders and senior pastors of HRock Church in Pasadena, California. Having traveled to over 55 nations, Che ministers at conferences on healing, revival and reformation. He is President of Harvest International Ministry, an apostolic network with over 10,000 churches in more than 45 nations. He is also International Chancellor of Wagner Leadership Institute. Che has authored 13 books, writes for **Ministry Today** Magazine and hosts his own television program, "The Holy Spirit Today."

Sue directs children's ministries and is committed to pouring a biblical foundation of the kingdom of God into the youth generation and making them disciples. Her passion includes building strong marriages and families, unlocking truths of identity in Christ, and releasing children and women into greater kingdom potential.

Che and Sue have been married for over 32 years. They have four adult children and recently welcomed their first grandson.

Joshua & Janet Angela Mills

Joshua and Janet Angela Mills are dedicated to bringing the love and glory of God to the nations of the earth.They worship and teach by standing under the cloud and ministering directly from the glory unto the people.

Joshua has authored over 20 books and written more than 600 worship songs that have been used by church congregations worldwide.

Janet Angela moves in a prophetic anointing and ministers the Word of faith at church meetings and conferences. An earmark of their ministry is the remarkable signs, wonders and creative miracles that the Holy Spirit performs while they simply teach and testify about the goodness of God. They have raised up more than 3,500 Miracle Workers around the world through their *Intensified Glory Institute*® spiritual training programs. Together, they have traveled all over North America and around the world, creating a realm of glory wherever they go. They have ministered to millions through radio, television and online webcasts. They currently reside in Vancouver, Canada, along with their two children.

Robert & Katie Souza

Robert Souza is the Operations Director of Expected End Ministries. His wife, Katie Souza, is Founder and President of EEM. She is an international speaker, television and radio host and author.

In February 2006, Katie completed her book, **The Captivity Series: The Key to Your Expected End.** It is being read or taught in hundreds of facilities across the US and the world.

In late 2006, the Lord released a healing anointing on Expected End Ministries. Robert oversees every aspect of the ministry so that his wife, Katie, can continue to travel across the nation teaching how the Glory Light of Jesus can heal soul wounds enabling the Body of Christ to walk in wholeness and freedom. The Lord has called EEM to start a discipleship program for ex-felons coming out of prison. This program, The Transformation House, will be located in Pinal County, Arizona. www.ExpectedEndMinistries.com

Bart & Kim Hadaway

Bart serves as a pasto-
ral and spiritual overseer
with XP Ministries in Maricopa, Arizona. He carries
and releases the love of
the Father everywhere he
goes. He has a true pas-
tor's heart coupled with
a keen prophetic insight.
Bart teaches, preaches and
ministers in a powerful re-

vival anointing, impacting individual lives as well as the regions
he goes into. Lives are transformed spiritually, emotionally and
physically by the love and power of the Holy Spirit as he ministers.

Kim currently serves as head intercessor for XP Ministries in
the U.S. She, too, has a pastor's heart, desiring to see the love
of Christ consume and transform people. She believes all in the
body of Christ are called to be ministers of fire! Kim leads wom-
en's groups and intercessory prayer, as well as teaching, preaching and operating in a strong seer anointing. She has seen the
Lord impact people and regions through prayer and the release
of the prophetic.

HROCKCHURCH
CONNECTING COMMUNITY
ADVANCING PEOPLE

WWW.HROCKCHURCH.COM

A multi-ethnic, multi-generational, Holy Spirit filled church that is called to have a transforming impact in the city and society we serve.

Pastors Ché & Sue Ahn

COMMUNITY

MISSION

HARVEST INTERNATIONAL MINISTRIES

WWW.HARVESTIM.ORG

Harvest International Ministries (HIM) is a global network over 10,000 like-minded churches, ministries and missionaries committed to loving and helping each other fulfill the Great Commision.

WAGNER
LEADERSHIP INSTITUTE

WWW.WAGNERLEADERSHIP.ORG

EDUCATION

Wagner Leadership Institute is an international network of apostolic training centers established to equip the saints for kingdom ministry.

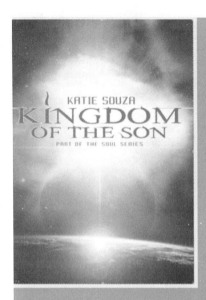

KINGDOM OF THE SON

Katie Souza, founder and President of Expected End Ministries, will release healing and show you how to position yourself to receive miracles in your own body, soul, and finances.

Learn how Holy Communion is used to heal soul wounds in an accelerated manner!! These teachings are in continuation of *The Soul Series!*

7 CD set includes Soaking CD

THE HEALING SCHOOL

Katie Souza has *re-mastered and updated* this teaching of the *Soul Series.* It is full of cutting edge, fresh revelation! Learn how demonic kings cause physical diseases, mental disorders, and financial lack but learn how to overcome and become a carrier of King Jesus. Move into the supernatural and receive your healing!!

7 CD or DVD sets include Activation

Expected End Ministries
Transforming Captivity into Promise

P.O. Box 1289 ~ Maricopa AZ ~ 85139
560.568.7600- Main   560.568.9961-Prayer Line
www.ExpectedEndMinistries.com

LIVING IN EXPECTANCY

Excitement is great. But God wants us to move beyond excitement and into expectancy. Excitement stirs us up to believe for the things of God. But expectancy latches on to His promises, refusing to settle for anything less. Expectancy is what draws heaven to earth. It is what propels hope into faith. It is what crosses us over into the Promised Land of His exceeding, great and precious promises fulfilled!

In this stirring message, Bart Hadaway teaches you how to move past excitement into expectancy. As you listen, you will feel your spirit leap as it grabs hold of this revelation, soaring to new heights of faith... and new manifestations of His realized promises!

EXTREME DECREES FOR EXTREME TIMES

By Patricia King, Bart and Kim Hadaway Paulette Reed, and Robert Hotchkin

During challenging times of change and upheaval, there is one constant you can always rely on – God! He never changes. His promises are always yes and amen. And His word never fails!

In this book, Patricia King and her team have crafted a collection of EXTREME DECREES for EXTREME TIMES - truths and teachings that culminate in prophetic expressions of God's heart for you. Each Extreme Decree powerfully reminds you who you are to God, who He is for you, and the inexhaustible blessings of heaven that have been given to you through the cross. As you read through these declarations of God's truth and love, your faith will be stirred and your spirit will be strengthened as you are reminded that you are extremely loved, extremely blessed, and extremely empowered to put a faith-filled demand on heaven for your circumstances to align with God's heart for you in every situation in your life!

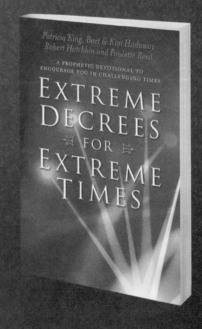

DAN & LINDA WILSON
The Joy of Spirit-Led Intimacy

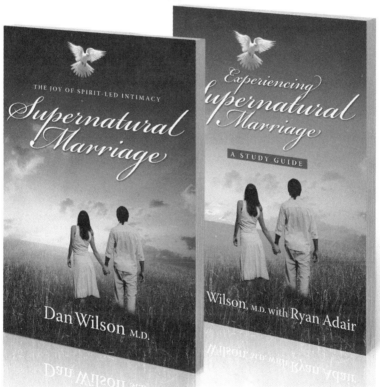

Now Available in Spanish!

Additional copies of this book may be purchased
through SupernaturalMarriage.org
and the contributing authors' ministries.

Additional copies of this book and other book titles
from XP Publishing are also available at XPmedia.com

BULK ORDERS: We have wholesale prices for stores and
ministries. Please contact: usaresource@xpmedia.
In Canada: resource@xpmedia.com

Our books are also available to bookstores through
Anchordistributors.com

www.XPPublishing.com
A Department of XP Ministries